# KINDERGARTEN ▼ BASICS

# KINDERGARTEN ▼ BASICS

KATE KELLY AND ANNE ZEMAN

ILLUSTRATION BY CHRIS REED

BOOK DESIGN BY ALLEYCAT DESIGN, INC.

## THE TASHUA-PRINCETON STUDY GROUP

Jacqueline Norcel

Brian Lally

Allida Finnegan

Jean Marie Mysogland

Janice Coulson

Terry Buckingham

Judy Gallo

Lorraine Dattner

Kate Kelly

Anne Zeman

BLACK DOG & LEVENTHAL PUBLISHERS • NEW YORK

Published by

Black Dog & Leventhal Publishers, Inc.
151 West 19th Street
New York, New York  10011


Distributed by

Workman Publishing Company
708 Broadway
New York, New York  10003

Manufactured in the United States of America

ISBN:  1-884822-11-8

For Kendra, who inspired and mastered the basics.

# ACKNOWLEDGMENTS

Many thanks to the teachers, counselors, parents, and children who read, responded to, and tested the activities in this and the other *Basics* books, especially: Kendra, Erin, Megan, Maura, Bill, Alanna, Keara, Brooke, Amber, and the student body of Tashua School.

Thanks, too, to Mary Jo Battistelli and Sovanni Bun for getting the manuscripts together, to Pam Horn, a patient editor with a kind blue pencil, and to J.P. Leventhal for believing in *Basics*.

# CONTENTS

# FOREWORD

As a teacher for thirty-five years, I realize that vision, commitment, and education count most at the family and community levels. Only through the enduring partnership of families, educators, and other dedicated citizens can America's learning enterprise—our local schools—unleash our children's full potential.

Until the completion of high school, a child spends only thirteen percent of his or her waking hours in school—so it is logical that activities outside of school have a dramatic impact on learning. Numerous studies focusing on the home-school connection have shown that parents' active support of a child's education can add as much as half a year's progress to every school year.

The *Basics* series is designed to help parents support the educational process through projects and activities that sharpen skills, focus goals, and provide a sense of accomplishment. And learning has never been so much fun. With *Basics*, you enter into the process right along with your kids, demonstrating the pleasure and importance of reading, writing, and mathematics in everyday life. And when you instill a love of learning, you lay the groundwork for your child's entire future.

Remember, children develop and learn in many different ways, and at different rates. All children have ups and downs in learning. Your support and encouragement—and your participation—are key to insuring your child's continuing development.

Parents can be extraordinary teachers. I invite you to use *Basics* to help your child identify strengths, set realistic goals, and discover his or her true potential.

Jacqueline J. Norcel
Principal, Tashua School

*Jacqueline J. Norcel, Chair of the Tashua-Princeton Study Group and Principal of Tashua School in Trumbull, Connecticut, holds B.S. and M.S. degrees in education, as well as an Ed.D. degree. She is the recipient of numerous professional awards and service commendations, including the National Distinguished Principals Award. Under her stewardship, Tashua School was named a National Exemplary School by the United States Department of Education.*

*Since 1985, Ms. Norcel has served as Adjunct Professor in the Department of Education at Sacred Heart University in Connecticut, and has written articles, speeches, and lectures on primary education and parent-teacher collaboration in education.*

# KINDERGARTEN BASICS

## INTRODUCTION

W hy can't Johnny read? Why are our children outpaced in math and sciences by the youth of other developed and emerging nations? What has brought about the decline of education in our country?

Over the past several years, these questions have fuelled considerable debate among educators, psychologists, anthropologists, social historians, politicians, and parents. Johnny can't read because classroom standards have slipped away in our public schools. But how can our teachers compete when budget cuts leave them with unwieldy class sizes and spare, inferior, or obsolete materials?

Among the consequences of our national concern about the state of education is a proliferation of books and articles pinpointing various reasons for and solutions to the problem. Popular among the reasons proferred is that, because our children suffer from a lack of common background coming into school and this lack continues because of differences in state-to-state curricula, our children can't be educated efficiently. The suggested solution lies in providing our children with more culturally and educationally uniform backgrounds from preschool through the primary grades. This philosophy has spawned a popular series of books for parents and teachers, a series that attempts to outline what the elements of a uniform educational program are.

But many parents and teachers reject the notion of educational uniformity, emphasizing instead the need for diversity and multiculturalism in education. Proponents of multicultural approaches often argue that, in order to break down the barriers of prejudice and misunderstanding, diversity must be taught, that acceptance comes through knowledge and awareness.

In the meantime, who's supposed to be teaching? If our children aren't learning in school, should our children be schooled in the home? Is it incumbent on parents with school-age children—even those in the best of school systems and with the most promising academic futures—to evaluate their children's academic progress and tutor them in their curricular subjects?

The *Basics* series doesn't attempt to answer these questions, nor does it represent an approach to solving the problems in American education. Instead, *Basics* is geared to reinforce fundamental learning skills—skills above debate and widely embraced as essential to success in school. The series is written on the premise that parents should not have to be teachers, but that parents can and should introduce and reinforce learning by encouraging their children to play skill-related games and activities.

Rather than extend the classroom into the kitchen, keep the the kitchen for family fun. Games and activities exercise the critical-thinking, problem-solving, and other curriculum-related skills essential to your child's success in school. You don't need a teaching certificate or a degree in education to help your child learn. You simply need interest in your child's education and the time and simple materials to encourage productive play.

# WHY BASICS?

*Basics* in the series title refers to basic learning skills, skills that despite the debate and controversy in education are recognized as fundamental, and skills that are encouraged and developed in the school program. Ideally, home learning is consistent with the school program. But at home as well as at school, effective learning combines several characteristics:

- Learning is an active, not a passive process. Children learn better from doing and telling than by being told.

- Learning comes naturally from experience. Real-life experiences are the best basis for learning.

- Learning has a holistic nature. The process is based on mastering foundational systems rather than focusing on specific, small tasks.

- Learning comes from activities and games that meet a child's needs and interests.

- Learning involves making choices.

- Learning motivates interaction with people and materials, develops self-reliance and attention span.

## BASICS AND GRADE LEVELS

To foster age-appropriate skill development, the *Basics* series is divided into volumes based on grade levels. This method provides an easy reference point and, for the most part, will guide you to the appropriate volume for you and your child. Within each volume, skills sets are the topics of individual chapters. Within these chapters, activities become progressively more complicated. The objective is to introduce a skill, reinforce it, and then make using it challenging and fun. Although a child may be unable to do activities at the beginning of a school year, he or she will be better able by year's end. Some activities almost certainly require parental guidance and supervision. These activities are accompanied by a parent icon.

Although the *Basics* volumes outline a variety of activities for different interests and abilities, be sure the *Basics* volume you choose is appropriate. This is especially important in the early primary grades, where physical and mental development can vary widely from one child to the next. Your child may not be ready for the activities in his or her "grade level" *Basics* book, or may be ready for the next "grade level."

## BASICS, YOU, AND YOUR CHILD

The texts in all the *Basics* volumes address the child, not the parent. The introductions and chapter overviews, however, describe the learning skills emphasized and the particular purpose of each activity for the parent. Consequently, *Basics* books are written for both children and parents. While providing a guidebook for fun, they also provide a thumbnail of grade-specific learning objectives.

## DOWN TO BASICS

The activities and games in *Basics* require only simple materials—pencils, paper, cardboard, markers, paints, and recycled household materials. The purpose of limiting supplies is to make the activities easy and accessible to as wide an audience as possible. For those fortunate enough to have them, other materials-building systems, such as Lego® or Tinker Toys®, Colorforms®, two- and three-dimensional puzzles, modelling clays, etc.—are wonderful for creative learning. So, too, are cameras, calculators, and computers and the myriad educational software programs on disks and CD-ROM. Many of the *Basics* activities can be adapted to these materials, and much of the computer learning software available concentrates on developing many of the same skills.

In addition to the activities, each *Basics* book includes a section listing "Good Books to Read." These lists were compiled by the Tashua-Princeton Study Group. The criteria for selection included awards (Caldecott, Newbury, etc.), popularity among school children, availability (in print), and frequency of appearance on selected school and public library recommended reading lists. It is by no means comprehensive, but introduces a variety of authors and titles appropriate to early primary readers and listeners. Reading is essential to success in every school subject. Foster a love of reading in your child by reading to him or her as often as possible. Continue family reading throughout the school grades.

# IS IT A BIRD? IS IT A PLANE?

## SORTING

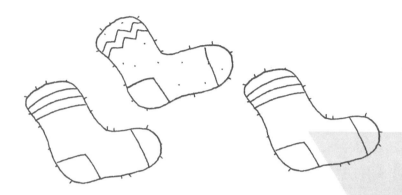

Sorting skills are fundamental to learning reading and math. By the time your child enters kindergarten, he or she may have had a great deal of experience sorting shapes, colors, sizes, numbers, and even categories and opposites. But there's no such thing as too much sorting. In kindergarten, your child's ability to sort will be reviewed and reinforced as a preparation for reading and math in the first grade.

Keep track of your child's sorting development. Follow our suggested activities to help your child develop and enhance basic sorting skills. As one sorting activity is mastered, introduce a new, more challenging activity.

# 1. SHAPE UP

By the end of the kindergarten year, most children are able to recognize basic geometric shapes. They are also able to sort these shapes—even if they are not shown in identical sizes or proportions.

The goal in "Shape Up" is to eliminate the "square peg in the round hole" problem. Play with shapes to help your child recognize, name, and sort them. Start with three shapes: circle, square, triangle. As your child masters these shapes, add one or two new shapes to your activities; rectangle and star, for example.

The activities in "Shape Up" call for eyes, an imagination, and, later, pencil and paper. However, some of the best activities for learning shapes can be found in the toy box. Blocks often come in a variety of different shapes. Colorforms®, too, present shapes in bright colors.

If you have blocks or Colorforms®, use them along with the principles of "Shape Up" to create new activities. Build a house, construct a dog, or erect a monument out of blocks. Create a landscape of Colorform® shapes.

If you don't have blocks or Colorforms®, check your closets or storage bins. Old boxes, gift paper towels, styrofoam balls, and cardboard circles from pizza boxes can be transformed into building materials for marvellous sculptures. Build a castle or a car—and help your child recognize, name, and sort shapes along the way.

# 2. COLOR KEY

Recognizing, naming, and sorting colors is also a skill most kindergartners practice and, with some help, master by year's end. Colors are everywhere. So are opportunities for naming and sorting colors. For example, as you take a walk with your child, pick up a leaf that has fallen from a tree. What color is the leaf? What about the leaves on the next tree along your route? Are the leaves the same color? What about the leaves on these trees as spring turns to summer and summer to fall. How many different colors are there on one tree?

## 3. PATTERN PLAY

"Pattern Play" takes the concepts in "Shape Up" and builds on them. Consequently, "Pattern Play" includes activities that are a bit more difficult than these in "Shape Up" but activities that nevertheless reinforce the sorting skills most kindergartners develop over the school year.

"Stained Glass" is a creative activity, but one that requires adult help and supervision. Many kindergartners will need some help creating the window border and even cutting the shape from the stiff poster board.

## 4. NOT QUITE ALIKE

Part of sorting is recognizing how things differ. In the first three activities in this chapter, the focus is on recognizing sameness. "Not Quite Alike" emphasizes difference.

In addition to the illustrations provided in the book, find or draw some of your own or use other sorting activities already prepared. Many children's magazines include "which doesn't belong?" and "which is different?" activities. Guide your child through these or find illustrations in books and magazines that show differences.

Remember, start simple. Your kindergartner isn't going to master *Where's Waldo* in one sitting. Setting up too difficult an activity may actually discourage your child and disengage him or her from playing sorting games.

## 5. RAG SHOP

Why not transform dreary chores into sorting fun? Try "Rag Shop."

Sorting clothes and recyclables is fun—if it's not too difficult. Start with two or three sorting categories, then add more as your child masters the first few. Picture clues are always helpful. Also, limit the quantity of things to sort and keep the timeframe short—say, five to ten minutes. Otherwise, the game will once again seem to be a chore. Even the most obvious sorting errors—a black sock among white T-shirts, for example—are bound to happen. Sorting skills are far from fine-tuned in most kindergartners.

## 6. TRICKS WITH TREATS

Unless you're pressed for time, make trips to the grocery store, a.k.a. "Sorting Gallery." You'll have to use your discretion as to what your kindergartner can gather for you, and how many piles the grocery cart can hold. But, with some simple guide-lines, let your child test his or her sorting skills in the challenging grocery store arena.

Because your child probably can't read, be sure to guide the grocery gathering until you're certain your child knows what your brand looks like. Also, take the opportunity to explain how the grocery store is "sorted"—produce aisle, meat and dairy cases, deli, bakery, etc.

As with any sorting activity, start simple. Ask your child to sort items into two or three piles to start, then add categories.

A note on "Price Piles": Many kindergartners have little or no concept of money, and most likely no experience of reading the numbers on a price tag or label. So, to play "Price Piles," you'll need to tell your child how much an item costs—to the nearest dollar—and let your child sort from there. Many activities have stressed sorting things by difference or category. "Price Piles" introduces the idea of sorting by greater than and less than.

# 7. REDECORATE

In "Redecorate," your child is asked to sort items into more categories than in other activities in the book. But all the items are familiar and easily referenced within the walls of your home.

Be sure to guide your child through the planning of "A Room With A View." Establish a size parameter for drawings so they are large enough to be cut out, but small enough to fit into the poster "house."

You may want to play "What's Wrong with This Picture" with your child, first involving yourself in the creation of the poster house, then setting up the first trick house. Your child can then use the items you've created together to play "What's Wrong with This Picture" with his or her friends, or play "A Room With A View" alone.

# SHAPE UP

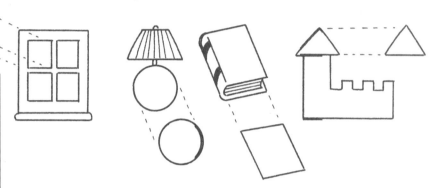

L ook around you. What do you see?
If you're indoors, you might see rugs, lamps, tables, and chairs, or cabinets, countertops, stoves, sinks, and windows. If you're outdoors, you might see houses, fences, rooftops, door frames, and roadways, or trees, shrubs, boulders, and birds.

## THE SHAPE OF THINGS

**circle**

Now think about simple shapes, for example, squares, rectangles, triangles, circles, and ovals.

Can you imagine *building* all the things around you from these shapes?

**quadrilateral**

**rectangle**

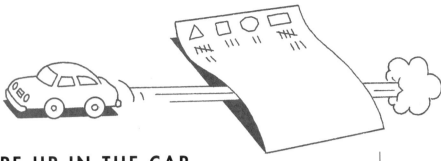

# SHAPE UP IN THE CAR

You can play "Shape Up" on car trips. All you need to do is find shapes in the landscapes outside the car window. For example, you might say, "That speed limit sign is a rectangle," or, "That roof makes a triangle."

Make "Shape Up" even harder by keeping score. Draw a variety of shapes on a scratch sheet to form a score card. Then, draw a hash mark beside the drawings of the shapes you see. Look at the drawing above to see what your score card might look like.

Play as long as you like. You could decide to play for a number of minutes or for a number of miles traveled. When you're done playing, simply add up your hash marks and see who's seen the most shapes.

square

# ART SCHOOL

Drawing pictures of people, dogs, cats, and other things can be made easier by looking at them as collections of basic shapes. You can improve your art skills and maybe even draw a masterpiece.

triangle

**You'll need:**
paper • pencils • crayons or markers
• ruler or straight edge

star

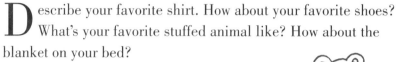
# COLOR KEY

D escribe your favorite shirt. How about your favorite shoes? What's your favorite stuffed animal like? How about the blanket on your bed?

When you describe these treasured things, do you mention their colors? Do you have a favorite color? Are any or all of your treasures made in your favorite color?

Just how important are colors? Sort some out and then decide.

## COLOR MY WORLD

Play a game of "Color My World" to see if you and your friends know your colors.

**You'll need:**
**contruction paper of many colors or white paper**
**• crayons or markers**

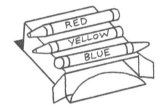

## DOUBLE YOUR COLORS?

## AN EXPERIMENT

**Even the smallest box of crayons contains all the basic colors:**

**red • yellow • blue**

*and*

**orange • green • purple**

First, sort out one sheet of each color of construction paper, or color a different colored patch on each of several sheets of white paper to make a set of color flashcards.

Then, test yourself on the cards.

Next, test your friends. Flash the colors quickly, one by one. See how many colors your friends can name in one round through the cards.

You can make an even more interesting game out of "Color My World." First, find some friends or family to put to the test.

Then, show one color to each player and ask what comes to mind. For example, you might think of a wagon when you see the color red, but someone else might think of a fire truck. Because you're moving through the cards quickly, some answers might seem pretty silly. Be sure to stop for a laugh!

## PAINT A NEW FAIRY TALE

What if the sky were yellow, the grass orange, and the leaves on the trees grew pink and purple? Would you be wandering around in some alien backyard on a strange planet? Possibly . . . but you'd probably just be playing "Paint a New Fairy Tale."

**You'll need:**
watercolor or tempera paints • brushes • water • manila paper or heavy stock • newspapers or protective covering for work area

If you mix red and yellow, you'll make orange. Yellow mixed with blue makes green. And blue mixed with red makes purple.

Sometime when you have your paint set out, try mixing red, yellow, and blue in these different combinations. You'll double your colors—and more!

First, prepare your work area. Be sure to protect your work surface so spilled paints or water won't ruin a tabletop or work-space. Open your paints, wet your brushes, and be sure you have a cup or two of rinse water prepared for the brushes, too.

Then, think of a scene from a fairy tale. You might want to look at the pictures in your favorite book. Notice how the characters are dressed. Look at the buildings, carpets, furniture, or the bright colors of the landscapes.

For example, you might study a scene with a wicked witch holding a broomstick. The sky is dark and forbidding behind her. In the scene, the witch's dress is certainly black, her skin is possibly pale green with lots of ugly warts.

When you've got your scene well in mind, paint it.

Next, paint the scene again, but use different colors.

What if the witch has lovely skin—no warts to be seen—her dress is pink, and the sky is blue behind her.

Last, compare your two pictures. How has color changed your paintings?

# PATTERN PLAY

Have you played "Shape Up" (see p. 14)? In that game, you try to find basic shapes in the objects around you. Why not play a quick round to freshen your memory.

Now, let's make "Shape Up" a little bit different. Look carefully at the shapes around you. Within any one shape, are there smaller shapes? Do the shapes work with other shapes to form even larger shapes? Are the smaller shapes set down in the same way each time? If so, the shapes form patterns.

## STAINED GLASS

Create a pattern and change it into a stained glass window.

**You'll need:**
drawing paper • pencil • crayon or marker • colored tissue paper • tape or glue • construction paper or poster board • scissors • tape or a tack

You can draw shapes and then put them together to create a pattern.

First, draw several shapes in different sizes on a piece of drawing paper. Draw lots of triangles, squares, circles, stars. Don't worry about making all the lines straight. Just make lots of shapes.

Then, cut out the shapes and fit them together like puzzle pieces on top of a piece of construction paper or poster board. Trace around the shapes and cut them out of the poster board.
Next, cut pieces of colored tissue paper to cover the holes in the construction paper. Glue or tape the tissue paper in place.

Last, turn over the poster board. You've made a beautiful stained glass window!

# USE YOUR NOODLE

Make a pattern with macaroni. Any type of pasta will do. Just use your noodle and create beautiful patterns.

**You'll need:**
**dried pasta in various shapes or colors • food coloring (optional) • glue • paper plates or poster board • string or thread**

Be sure your work area is protected from glue spills!

Then, make a pattern with the pasta shapes you've selected. You can arrange your pattern on a paper plate or on some poster board. Once you've got a pattern in mind, glue the pasta shapes down.

Next, let your pasta creations dry thoroughly and enjoy your pasta art.

For a variation, select pastas that are tube-shaped or wheel-shaped. These pastas can be strung on string or thread. Simply string your pasta pattern and you'll have created macaroni jewelry. Now that's really using your noodle!

# NOT QUITE ALIKE

S ometimes things aren't exactly as they seem. You might look at the picture below and see three stars. They appear to be just the same. Or do they?

Now, look at these drawings of a day at the beach (at left). Are they the same? If they're not, how are they different?

Now you might say all beaches look the same. The same goes for beach umbrellas. But even though a beach is a beach, one might have white sand, another black. The same holds true for the umbrellas. One might be striped and another spotted. So even things that are the same in one way can be different in others.

## FLASH!

You have to be quick, you have to look hard, because this game is over in a flash!

**You'll need:**
markers • construction paper or poster board to make
flashcards • scissors • glue or paste

Use sheets of construction paper or cut poster board into pieces of the same size to use as flashcards.

Then, divide each flashcard into two sections.

Next, draw the same picture on both sizes of the flashcard. On some cards, be sure the picture is absolutely the same in every detail. On other flashcards, make something a little different.

Last, test your friends to see if they can tell which flashcard pictures are not quite alike.

# RAG SHOP

Have you ever looked in your laundry hamper? What do you see? A big jumble of dirty shirts, smelly socks, worn underwear, and last week's pajamas, right?

## DIRTY CLOTHES

Have you ever noticed how your dirty clothes get washed? I'll bet the socks are washed in one load, the underwear in another. Play clothes are separated from good clothes, and whites are sorted for a special load with bleach.

Ask if you can help sort the wash. Find out what piles to make and try to fit your dirty clothes into clothes-washing categories.

## FRESH FROM THE WASHER

Want to be even more helpful with the laundry? Ask if you can help sort the clean clothes. Socks are especially good to sort. Find the two socks that belong together and make pairs to put in your drawers. You can also sort your shirts from your shorts and your pajamas from your underwear.

# INTO THE DRAWERS

Do you wear snow pants in the summer? Swimsuits in the snow? Probably not.

If you live in a climate where you need warm sweaters and pants in winter and lightweight play clothes for summer, you can take "Rag Shop" one step further. Ask if you can help sort one season's clothes from another.

Even if you don't have different clothes for different seasons, ask if you can sort your clothes by color and type.

**You'll need:**
**clothes • dresser drawers or other clothes storage areas**
**• paper (optional) • markers**

First, decide how many different types of clothes you have:

**underwear**
**socks**
**pajamas**
**shirts**
**shorts and slacks**
**sweaters**
**best clothes**

Then, sort your clothes into separate piles by type.

Next, decide where you'll store each type of clothing.

Last, put your nicely sorted clothes away in the places you've chosen. So you don't forget your great system, draw label-sized pictures to remind you where each different type of clothing belongs. Ask a parent to write the words to go with your pictures and see if it's okay to tape your labels in place.

## RECYCLING CENTER

Glass, some plastics, cans, and newspapers are recycled. That means the materials are used again. The idea of recycling is to save Earth's resources.

Ask about recycling. How does your family sort recyclable materials? Are your recyclables picked up or do you take them to a recycling center?

Once you understand the recycling system at your house, ask if you can be the family recycling manager. That means you take care of sorting and storing the recyclables.

# GROCERY GAMES

T̲ag along on a trip to the grocery store. There's so much to do. Of course, you can push the cart up the aisles or ride it down the rows. But everyone does that. So why not play something new? How'd you like to be Inspector General of Food Affairs for your family? Here's how you do it.

First, help gather together the items on the grocery list. Once three or more items are in the cart, separate them into different areas of the cart. You can sort in different ways:

| | | |
|---|---|---|
| **size:** | big | little |

*or*

| | | |
|---|---|---|
| **touch:** | hard | soft |

*or*

| | | |
|---|---|---|
| **type of packaging:** | cans | jars |
| | soft things | cold things |

*or*

| | | |
|---|---|---|
| **type of food:** | vegetables | fruits |
| | meats | cheeses |
| | bakery items | |

*or*

| | | |
|---|---|---|
| **size of package:** | small packages | large packages |
| | medium-sized packages | |

## SORTING SWEETS FOR SAFETY

It's Halloween. You and your friends are in your costumes and out in the neighborhood. "Trick or treat," you cry. With each door that opens, your treat bag becomes heavier with Halloween loot.

When you get home, sort your candy with your parents. You can separate lollipops from chocolate bars, gum from hard candy—whatever you wish.

Y ou could even sort by the color of the food or shape of its container. Or try this:

**good food**
**yucky food**
**not a food**

Each time you go grocery shopping, you can sort things differently.

Your job as Inspector General doesn't have to end at the grocery store check out line. Oh, no! Use your sorting skills in the kitchen when you arrive home. As the groceries come out of the shopping bags, sort them for storage. You may sort out cans for the cabinets, milk for the refrigerator, frozen yogurt for the freezer. When you get really good at your job as Inspector General, you can even sort for specific shelves or drawers in the pantry or the refrigerator.

# PRICE PILES

Once you've mastered Inspector General of Food Affairs, you might want to try a trickier grocery store game. In order to play "Price Piles," you sort grocery items by price. You might want an older person to help you at first, especially if you can't read the prices on the items. But after a few rounds of "Price Piles," you should have no trouble reading prices or setting your own rules.

To get started, try an easy round.

First, pick a rule for sorting. For example, you might decide to sort the groceries into two piles:

**items that cost more than $2**
**items that cost less than $2**

Then, put all the items that cost more than $2 in one part of the grocery cart and all the items that cost less in another part.

The better you come to understand prices, the more price categories you can use to sort "Price Piles."

**Just be sure you sort out any candy that is not completely wrapped. That means any homemade treats, such as popcorn balls or brownies, candies or nuts without wrappers, or candy with torn or open wrappers.**

**Once you've sorted your treats, make sure you throw away the pile of candies with torn wrappers or the treats that came without any packaging at all—unless your parents say the candy or treat is okay.**

# REDECORATE

Do you keep your toys in the freezer? Is there a refrigerator next to your bed? Is there a couch in your bathroom? Yes? Maybe it's time to redecorate!

## A ROOM WITH A VIEW

Here's a brain teaser to test your sorting skills and a fun activity to fill a rainy afternoon.

> **You'll need:**
> drawing paper • a pencil • crayons or markers (optional) • scissors • poster board • a marker • paste or glue

First, draw as many household items you can think of. Include furniture as well as plants, tabletop items, books, a bathtub, hangers, and anything else that belongs inside a house. If you're stumped, look around the house to get more ideas. If you feel like it, color the items you've drawn.

Then, cut out each item. Next, get some help to draw a marker outline of a house on the poster board, showing the outline for different rooms.

Last, paste down the cutouts to furnish the rooms of your poster house.

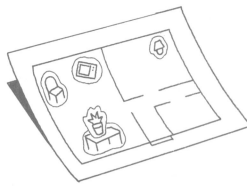

# WHAT'S WRONG WITH THIS PICTURE?

So you think you know where the furniture belongs in your house? Well, look again. See if you can spot what's wrong in the picture below.

Now, stump your friends. Create a trick house using the pieces you cut out to make "A Room with a View." Simply place one item in a room where it doesn't belong. For example, you might put a bathtub in the kitchen, or a bed in the garage. Then, show the poster. See who spots the problem (or problems) first.

# 2

# I THOUGHT IT WAS . . .

## ASSOCIATIONS

When your child associates one thing with another, your child is thinking critically. The ability to think critically is, like sorting, a fundamental logic skill, one that will serve as a basic ability in learning reading and math.

The activities in this chapter emphasize associations in different ways. Some activities ask your child to associate sameness, others difference.

# 1. THAT'S NOT A PLATE . . . IT'S A FLYING SAUCER

This set of activities is geared to promote creativity, while reinforcing and introducing the use and function of familiar objects.

"Inventor's Palace" is a very sophisticated activity for a kindergartner. Be prepared to offer considerable assistance with this project. It takes not only hard imaginative work, but also fairly refined sorting and organizing skills. Without your help, many kindergartners will be overwhelmed by the activity, make a terrible mess, or both.

# 2. SISTERS, COUSINS, AND AUNTS

"Family Units" reinforces association and sorting skills by practicing differentiation. Although most children associate the word sister with a female, for example, they also need to differentiate one sister from another.

If you have a large family—immediate or extended—your child will probably be familiar with family names and associations. If you don't have a big family to draw on for examples, talk about family associations from favorite story books or movies.

"Not Quite Identical Twins" teaches same and different concepts using a variety of examples. Even if you think same and different associations are obvious, ask your child what he or she sees. You may need to guide your child to observe what makes different things similar and similar things different.

"Print Shop" takes the same and different lessons of "Not Quite Identical Twins" into (literally) a hands-on activity. Your child will probably have more fun from getting hands in paint than in learning association skills. But draw your child into the purpose of the activity. You may want to point out, for example, that no one shares the same fingerprints. Maybe you'd be willing to commit your digits to the paint can to prove the point!

"Fantasy Families" allows children to create their own ideal associations—or comical, nonsensical, or practical associations. If you encourage your child in this activity, don't expect to complete several pictures in one day. Instead, create a fantasy family, leave the project for a while, then do another.

## 3. ZOO STORY

In this set of activities, your child uses logic to group or associate obviously different things.

"Members Only, Please!," although simple at face value, offers a challenge for the whole family. It all depends on the topic. When you play with your kindergartner, try to keep the zoo theme simple—for example, colors in a small box of crayons—then, gradually make the game more difficult—for example, colors in a large box of crayons.

"A Zoo in a Box" is too difficult for most kindergartners to build alone! This is surely an activity wherein you're the architect and your child the design consultant!

## 4. BIG, BIGGER, BIGGEST

By kindergarten, most children are proficient in the language and meaning of many associations: "He got more ice cream!" "Can't I stay up later?" "I'm the smallest in my class."

In "Big, Bigger, Biggest," basic comparative associations and vocabulary are reinforced and introduced. Then they are applied in "Simple Coin Toss." While "Simple Coin Toss" is fairly straightforward for kindergartners to play, "Advanced Coin Toss" is not. Your child will almost certainly need help—not only in creating the game board, but also in playing and scoring.

## 5. UP, DOWN, IN, OUT, UNDER, OVER, AND THROUGH

This set of activities reinforces and introduces opposites. Both "The Opposites Game" and "Quick Draw" can be played virtually anywhere, anytime—except, perhaps, in the car if you're driving! Once your child has the hang of it, he or she can play with friends and leave you to navigate other skills.

Diptyches are not intended as car games—nor are they easy for a kindergartner to assemble. Be sure to help prepare and put together diptyches with your child.

## 6. CONFOUND IT!

Free association games are fun—no matter what your age or grade level. Starting your kindergartner on some free associations sharpens logic skills early.

In this set of activities, simple free associations are followed by two more difficult activities: "Confounding Questions" and "Confuse-athon." Don't be surprised if your kindergartner has a hard time at first. Try to explain the illogic of the questions. If it's simply too hard to be fun, save the activity for another week. Then try again. It may take weeks, months, even years for a child to comprehend these brain teasers. Only a very precocious child will grasp these activities early on.

# THAT'S NOT A PLATE . . . IT'S A FLYING SAUCER

When you see a bowl, you know it's a dish for foods like soup or cereal. When you see a glass, you know it's for drinks. A chair is for sitting on and a bathtub is for soaking in. Boxes are containers for holding books, shoes, toys, and other treasures. Doors are for going in and out, trash bags hold the household trash. Knives and forks are for eating with, bedsheets are for sleeping on. All around you are many, many things—each with its own particular use or job to do.

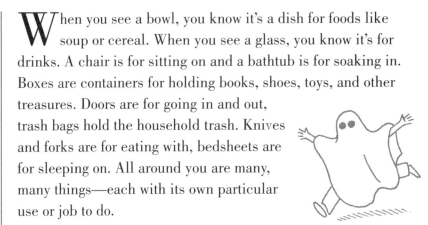

Now, imagine you've never seen a bowl or a chair, a fork or a bedsheet. What could these strange objects be? What are they called? What are they used for?

A bowl might be a special type of rain hat, big bowls for people, little bowls for dolls. And what name might these rain hat bowls have? Umbowlas? Bowlbrellas?

Think of some other ordinary things. How would you use them in new ways? You'll need a good imagination.

You might want to draw some of your brilliant ideas or ask your parents to help you make a list of the things you think of. If you keep a record, you'll have an easy time putting together an Inventor's Palace (see right).

**You'll need:**
drawing paper or scrap paper • pencil, crayon, or marker • pencil

## FRISBEES

**Frisbees are flying everywhere, from playgrounds and parks to beaches and resorts. So what's a Frisbee™? It looks like a flying saucer, only tinier. And it flies like a flying saucer. So did it come from outer space or was it a gift to earthlings from a generous alien creature? No.**

# INVENTOR'S PALACE

Display the imaginative delights you've created from everyday objects in an Inventor's Palace. The Palace is a type of museum you can set up in your bedroom, basement, or garage.

**You'll need:**
a large room • paper tags for labels • a pencil • a collection of things to display

First, look around the house or the garage for everyday objects that just might be put to a new use. If you made drawings of new uses for things or had your folks make a list for you, move to the next step.

Then, gather up the things you need to build your inventions and take them to the Palace. Set up the inventions and try to show how they are to be used. If a paper plate is now a flying saucer, put some toy aliens next to it.

Next, draw picture labels to show how the inventions work.

Last, invite your friends and neighbors to visit the Inventor's Palace— a dreamer's paradise for sure!

Frisbees were invented by students at Yale College. But the first Frisbees weren't made out of brightly colored plastic and purchased in the toy store. Instead, the students tossed upside down aluminum pie plates in what became a new-fangled game of catch. They called the pie plates "Frisbees," and a new toy was born!

Come to think of it, an upside down Frisbee would make a great plate!

# SISTERS, COUSINS & AUNTS
## (OR BROTHERS, COUSINS & UNCLES)

Some things are always the same. Look at these pictures:

You know exactly what these things are. But are all hands, dogs, and bicycles really the same? Take a closer look.

## FAMILY UNITS

Each one of us is special in our own way. And each one of us is part of a larger special group called a family. For example, we all have some kind of family—brothers, sisters, moms, dads, aunts, uncles, stepparents, cousins, and so on.

Now, each family is different from every other, even though the family members have the same names. Ask a school friend if she has a mom or dad, or if your pal at soccer camp has some uncles or cousins.

But are all relationships really the same?

As human beings, we're all part of an even larger family called humankind. Humankind includes only people—no fish, no dogs or cats, no birds, no dinosaurs. But while we're part of one family, we're all very different.

# NOT QUITE IDENTICAL TWINS

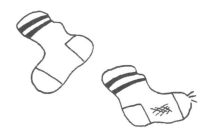

Many things come in pairs, for example, mittens, shoes, and socks. These pairs are kind of like twins. They belong together. The same goes for ears, eyeballs, nostrils, arms, legs, hands, and feet.

Take a look at a pair of your shoes. Are both shoes the same? Not quite, right? One fits the left foot, the other fits the right foot.

Now, take a look at a pair of your socks. Are they both the same? Probably—except for maybe a dirty spot or worn patch.

# PRINT SHOP

Set up a print shop to test your ideas about not quite identical twins.

**You'll need:**
a tarp, garbage bags laid flat, or newspapers spread to protect print shop area • ink or tempera paints • pie plates or pans (to hold the paints) • stamps (use hands, bare feet, soles of old sneakers) • brown paper or large sheets of art paper • a bucket of soap and water and an old towel for cleanup

First, set up your print shop. Ask an older person to help you spread a tarp or newspapers to protect your work area from water and paint spills.

Then, lay out your paints in pans large enough for dipping your stamps into. For example, if your bare foot is too big to fit flat into a pie pan, select a larger pan for your paints. Also, lay out the brown paper for printing next to the paint pan.

Next, dip a foot, a hand, or a sneaker into the paint and press it on the brown paper. Then do the other foot, hand, or sneaker. Repeat the printing process with other items.

Last, study your prints. Are they the same or are they mirror images?

For a variation, try stamping only a left foot, hand, or sneaker sole on paper. Then press another sheet of paper on top of the wet stamped paint and carefully peel it off. You'll have created another not quite identical twin.

## FANTASY FAMILIES

How many things can you think of that are the same but still different? Do you have mixing bowls in your kitchen? Are all those bowls the same—exactly the same? Or is one bigger than the other, or maybe a different color?

What other things do you notice around your home or in your neighborhood that are the same but really different? The buildings are all buildings, but are they all the same? What about the windows? Take a look at the toothbrushes in the bathroom or the blankets on the beds.

Once you've looked around to find things that are the same but different, you'll be ready to create some fantasy families.

**You'll need:**
**drawing paper • pencils, crayons, or markers**

Choose one of the things you discovered was the same but different. Maybe you noticed toothbrushes in the bathroom. Now imagine the toothbrushes as a fantasy family, including, for example, mom and dad toothbrushes, a big sister toothbrush, a baby toothbrush, maybe even a pet toothbrush.

Then imagine the toothbrushes together in a typical family scene. What would the toothbrushes be doing? Having dinner? Playing in the park? Shopping at a grocery store? Pick an activity for your fantasy family.

Then, draw or color a picture of your fantasy family working or playing together. You might want to make a big project out of "Fantasy Families." Over the course of a week, drawing a little at time, draw several pictures of your fantasy family doing different things. Gather the pictures together to make a storybook.

# ZOO STORY

## A GOOD, OLD-FASHIONED GAME OF 20 QUESTIONS

Have you ever played 20 Questions? I bet your parents have. It's kind of like playing "Members Only, Please!" and it's a great game for passing time on a car trip or in a restaurant. You can play 20 Questions anywhere. Here's all you have to do:

Choose one person to be "it." The person who's "it" has to think of a person, place, or thing. Then "it" must describe the person, place, or thing by offering a specific clue. For example, "it" might say, "I'm thinking of something in a kitchen."

Have you ever been to a zoo? What animals can you see there? Think about it for a minute. A zoo means lions, tigers, seals, elephants, lizards, emus, peacocks, rhinos, monkeys, snakes, and more. By bringing all these very different animals together in one place, the animals become one special thing— zoo animals.

You can make your very own zoo. You might want to make a zoo of your favorite stuffed animals, dolls, or action figures. You could even create a rock zoo.

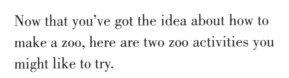

Now that you've got the idea about how to make a zoo, here are two zoo activities you might like to try.

# MEMBERS ONLY, PLEASE!

The next time you're waiting for a pizza or waiting for a movie, try a round of "Members Only, Please!" It's a zoo game in which you and your friends and family can create special zoos.

First, declare the type of zoo. For example, you might say:

**"I am building a zoo of things that are found in the ocean."**

Then, have each person take a turn naming one thing that would belong in the zoo. One person might say sand, another crabs, another octopuses, another seaweed. The last person to be able to name a zoo member wins the round. He or she can then name the next zoo.

Then, the other players ask "it" 20 questions to try to guess what "it" is thinking of. All 20 questions have to have "yes" or "no" answers. That means "it" only answers questions by saying "yes" or "no." Any other questions are ignored. For example, if "it" is thinking of something in a kitchen, you might ask, "Does it fit in a drawer?" or "Is it kept in the freezer?"If you can guess what "it" is thinking about in 20 questions or less, you get to be "it." If "it" stumps you after 20 questions, then "it" gets to think of a new person, place, or thing.

Sometimes a game of 20 Questions is hard to get organized. Be sure to ask your parents or some older friends to play with you and help keep you on track.

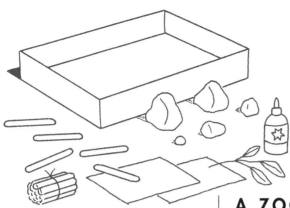

# A ZOO IN A BOX

Why not create "A Zoo in a Box?" You can group together some favorite items and tell how they are related.

**You'll need:**
**a box • markers and paper strips to make labels**
**• craft sticks • glue or paste • colored construction paper (green, brown, blue, etc.)**

First, decide the kind of zoo you want to build in the box. Maybe you'd like to build a zoo for your favorite rocks.

Then, gather together the items you'll need in the zoo. For example, gather all the different kinds of rocks you plan to include. Ask someone older to help you make labels for each item.

Next, you're ready to put your zoo together. Use craft sticks and glue to build "habitats" or "cages" for the zoo. Colored construction paper can be cut into shapes to show fields, hills, ponds, rivers, or other land features. Lay out the zoo—the construction paper, cages, and zoo items—in the box. Glue down the paper and cages, then attach the labels.

Now you've got "A Zoo in a Box" to show your friends and family!

# BIG, BIGGER, BIGGEST

I magine a tree. Now, imagine two trees together. Are they the same size? Or is one bigger than the other? Now, imagine three trees together. Are they all the same size? Is one the biggest of all? Is one taller than the other two? Is one wider?

Look at the trees on the right. Can you tell which tree is:

| big | *or* | small | wide | *or* | thin |
|-----|------|-------|------|------|------|
| **bigger** | | **smaller** | **wider** | | **thinner** |
| **biggest** | | **smallest** | **widest** | | **thinnest** |

| tall | *or* | short | close | *or* | far |
|------|------|-------|-------|------|-----|
| **taller** | | **shorter** | **closer** | | **farther** |
| **tallest** | | **shortest** | **closest** | | **farthest** |

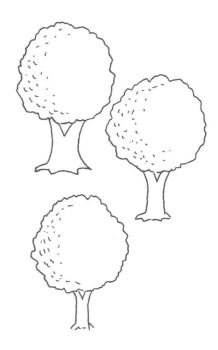

## SIMPLE COIN TOSS

Try a game of "Simple Coin Toss." You'll have fun and use your knowledge of relationships to keep score.

> **You'll need:**
> coins • a pail or basket

First, set down the pail or basket. Pace five steps back from the basket and set up a tossing line. If you're playing indoors or outside on grass, you could use a ruler or a piece of string to mark your tossing line. If you're playing outdoors, use sidewalk chalk on pavement or draw a line in the dirt with a stick.

Then, divide coins evenly among the players.

Next, have the players line up one by one. The first player determines where to toss the coins, for example:

**in the basket • past the basket • in front of the basket • on the right side of the basket • touching the outside of the basket**

Then, each player tries to toss one coin according to the call. When every player has tried, the one who best followed the call wins the round. That player makes the next call.

## CARNIVAL COIN TOSS

Have you ever been to a carnival where Coin Toss was played? The game involves throwing a coin—usually a nickel or a quarter—onto a table heaped with prizes. If your coin falls into a cup or into a painted circle, you win!

You can make your own version of "Carnival Coin Toss" in your favorite outdoor play area. Although you can improvise and play indoors or on a flat lawn or field, a sidewalk or driveway is probably the best place to set up your game.

**You'll need:**
20 or more pennies • 2 paper cups • poster board • 3 or more different colored markers or crayons • glue or tape • rocks • sidewalk chalk or an old bar of soap

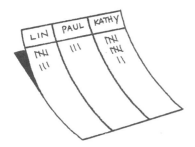

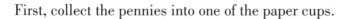

First, collect the pennies into one of the paper cups.

Then, create your game board using poster board and markers. You can make a standard target of circles within circles or you can make curious shapes. Be sure to use at least three different colors to create your poster board target and leave a space in the middle to glue or tape down the other paper cup. It will be the bull's-eye.

Next, set up your "Carnival Coin Toss" game. Place the target with the bull's eye cup flat on the floor or outside on a sidewalk or driveway. Use rocks to hold the target in place. Then, pace five steps back from the target and mark with chalk a line.

Now you're ready for a round of coin toss. Divide the pennies among the players. Then, one at a time, have each player stand behind the chalk line and toss the pennies toward the target. The object of the game is to get as many pennies as possible into the bull's eye or onto the highest scoring color areas. For example:

> **bull's-eye — 10 points**
> **red — 5 points**
> **blue — 3 points**
> **green — 1 point**

You can make up your own scoring system. Use your sidewalk chalk to keep score right next to your tossing line. Just be sure that inside the cup scores more than outside, and that nearest to the cup scores more than farthest from the cup.

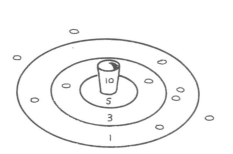

# UP, DOWN, IN, OUT, OVER, UNDER, AND THROUGH

**1.**

Black, white, bright, dark, yes, no. Do you know the name for pairs of words that mean something completely different? They're called *opposites*.

Can you identify these word pictures and their opposites? How'd you do?

**2.**

**4.**

**3.**

1) up — down    2) light — heavy    3) small — big    4) over — under

## OPPOSITES GAME

You've probably played the "Opposites Game" before. You say one thing but really mean the opposite. For example:

**I can't stand to eat ice cream!**

really means

**I love to eat ice cream!**

You can make it a little more interesting by adding a thought or two. For example:

**I can't stand to eat ice cream on a cold winter day!**

really means

**I love to eat ice cream on a hot summer day!**

Why not play a round of opposites on your next car trip. But be sure to explain what you're doing or you may sound a little odd!

## NOT!

Not is a special word. It helps make opposites and can be used in a variation on the "Opposites Game." In fact, "Not!" has become very popular and is played just about everywhere anytime. I bet you've played, too.

**I love liver and onions . . . <u>not</u>!**

## QUICK DRAW

See how quickly you and your friends can come up with opposites by playing "Quick Draw," a clapping game.

First, start a rhythm by clapping both hands on your thighs, then both hands together.

Then, recite the opening jingle:

> **Quick Draw! Quick Draw!**
> **Can you see**
> **If it's to be**
> **Or not to be?**

Next, the first player says a word, for example, "Up!" The player must say the word within two clapped beats. Then the next player has two clapped beats to answer with an opposite, for example, "Down!"

Play continues until a player misses a beat. If you're playing with more than two people, a player who misses is out of the game. Start over again by reciting the jingle. The player remaining after everyone else has missed wins the game.

## DIPTYCHES

In ancient times, writing tablets and pictures were created on hinged pieces of wood that would close to protect the work. When two panels fold over in this way, they are called diptyches.

Diptyches sometimes illustrate opposites, for example, good and bad or day and night. Why not create your own masterpiece in diptych to illustrate opposites?

**You'll need:**
**16 craft sticks • glue • felt • drawing paper • tempera or watercolor paints • brushes • a cup of water • newspapers spread to protect work area**

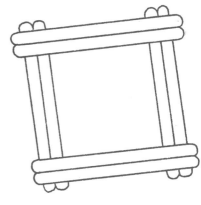

First, build the frame for your diptych using 16 craft sticks. Count out eight sticks and lay them out two by two to form a square panel, as shown.

Glue together where the craft sticks overlap. Now do the same thing with the remaining eight craft sticks.

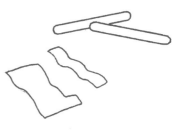

Then, cut two two-inch by half-inch strips of felt. Glue the felt strips to the outsides of the frames to form hinges.

Next, cut two pieces of drawing paper to fit into the frame. Be sure you cut the paper larger than the opening so you can glue the paper to the craft sticks when you've finished your painting. Once the paper is cut to size, paint your diptych. Be sure you illustrate opposites! And let your paintings dry completely.

Last, glue dry paintings into the diptych frames.

# CONFOUND IT!

## FREE ASSOCIATION

Have you ever played "Free Association?" One person says a word and another person says the first thing that the word brings to mind. For example, the first person might say "red," and the second person, "roses."

| | |
|---|---|
| **red** | **roses** |
| **stripes** | **tiger** |
| **furry** | **kitten** |
| **orange** | **juice** |
| **sun** | **moon** |

# CONFOUNDING QUESTIONS

**Is green your favorite color or do you like ice cream better?**

**Do you have a dog or does your sister take dance lessons?**

**Are you in kindergarten or does your brother play guitar?**

Did you notice anything wrong with the sentences you just heard? Did you think the ideas didn't quite fit together? If so, you're doing some sharp thinking.

# CONFUSE-ATHON

Think up a confusing question like those above. Then see if you can catch your friends. See how many try to answer your confusing questions. If a pal tells you your question is silly, let him or her in on the game. Then you can both start asking questions. Pretty soon you'll have a full-scale "Confuse-athon" going!

# 3

# ORDER IN THE COURT

## ORDER AND SEQUENCE

Although your kindergartner isn't asked to grapple with such sequence questions as, "Which came first, the chicken or the egg?" he or she will need to develop the logic skills that allow for proper ordering and sequencing of information. Order and sequence skills are implicit in reading and math, from such basic achievements as saying the alphabet or counting to 20.

# 1. ONCE UPON A TIME

These activities show beginning, middle, and end in storytelling, be it in books, movies, or anecdotes about real life.

Many kindergartners quickly recognize the proper sequence of pictures of their favorite bedtime stories. Drawing pictures in order might prove more difficult, however, and creating a filmstrip still harder. Help your child develop order and sequence skills by encouraging them to tell you stories. If your child wants to draw the stories for these activites, help him or her determine the most important beginning, middle, and end scenes to draw, or help list the various frames to make the filmstrip.

Even through the early primary years, children struggle to discern main points. If you can alleviate the need for your child to pull the main points from the literature, he or she will be free to focus on sequencing skills.


# 2. IF, THEN

In this section cause and effect relationships are explored. Because most kindergarteners haven't much experience of the world, keep the "If, Then" scenarios basic. Use the "I Say 'If'" game to introduce new ideas.

The activities in this section are good for play at home, outdoors—almost anywhere. Try a few rounds while you're waiting at the doctor's office or to fill the hours on a long car trip.

## 3. THE THIGH BONE'S CONNECTED TO THE KNEEBONE

These activities help your child solve sequence problems as if they were puzzles. You can also do "Skeleton Dance" to introduce some basic anatomy.

Unless your child is a precocious artist, drawing a skeleton is probably too difficult. Help your child draw the skeleton or trace one from a book. Or photocopy a Halloween version—or even provide a paper Halloween skeleton to take apart and put back together. But keep it simple.

## 4. DOMINOES

Dominoes are wonderful fun in addition to being effective learning tools. In these activities, dominoes are used to teach order and sequence. If you make your own dominoes, your child will also reinforce sorting and association skills. "Scoring Draw Dominoes," is a nice math exercise for older children, but is too difficult for most kindergartners. Nevertheless, expose your child to game scoring to provide them an incentive to learn more about counting and numbers.

"Domino Effect" shows cause and effect in sequence. The same skill can be demonstrated by building houses and towers out of playing cards—and toppling them. Be sure to help your child get started on these activities so they understand how to place and space the dominoes or playing cards.

# 5. THE ALPHABET SONG

Many kindergartners learn the alphabet song in school—or can already sing it by the time they enter school. Encourage your child to sing the song until he or she is knows it cold. Be sure l-m-n-o is understood as the sequence of four letters; some children think l-m-n-o is a word!

Once your child knows the "Alphabet Song," introduce "Alpha-claps"—easy version. Proceed to advanced "Alpha-claps." Use "Alpha-cards" to practice letter recognition while singing. Finally, see if your child and his or her friends can manage "Alpha-play."

# ONCE UPON A TIME

Every story has three basic parts: a beginning, a middle, and an end. Can you combine the pictures to "tell" the beginning, middle, and end of three of your favorite fairy tales?

**Three Little Pigs**

**Red Riding Hood**

**Hansel and Gretel**

You can tell your own stories in pictures.

**You'll need:**
drawing paper • pencils, crayons, or markers

Now, draw three pictures, one that tells the beginning, one that tells the middle, and one that tells the end of your story.

# AT THE MOVIES

Want to tell your picture stories in more detail? Create filmstrips.

**You'll need:**
**drawing paper • pencils, crayons, or markers**
**• a ruler • scissors • a shoebox • two dowels**
**(sticks or wrapping or kitchen paper tubes cut**
**down will do) • tape**

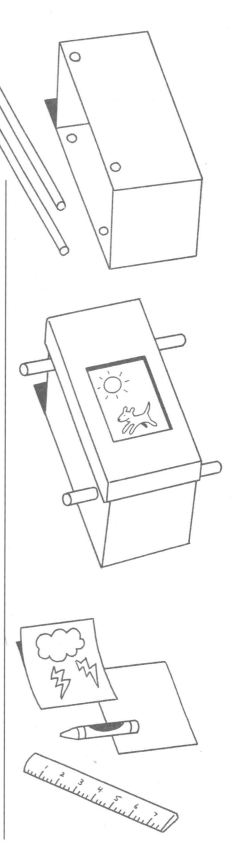

Mark and cut drawing paper into four inch by five inch pieces. Each piece will be one "frame" of your filmstrip. Be sure to leave the first and last frames blank. You may want to put the title of the story on the second frame. Mom or Dad can help you write it out.

Then, draw pictures on as may frames as you like to tell your story in pictures. Tape the frames together in order, attaching the frames from top to bottom—not side to side. Be sure to attach blank frames first and last!

Next, ask someone old enough to help, to cut a four-inch by five-inch hole in the top center of a shoebox, and two holes on each side to hold the dowels. Slide the dowels into place, then tape the filmstrip to the dowels.

Roll the dowels up and down to view the filmstrip.

# IF, THEN

If you are tired, then you rest. If you are hungry, then you eat. If you lose your favorite toy, then you are sad.

Many things fit together in an "if, then" way. Look at the pictures to the left. What happened first? Then what happened?

## I SAY "IF," YOU SAY "THEN"

You can play this "if, then" game with one other person or a whole roomful of folks. To start play, state an "if." You might say:

**If I were ruler of the world . . .**

or

**If I lived in Timbuktu . . .**

or

**If I had a new red wagon . . .**

or

**If my dog had fleas . . .**

or any other "if" that comes to mind.

If only two of you are playing, the other person provides the "then." If more than two of you are playing, point to the person you choose to answer the "if." He or she might answer the preceding "if" statements with:

**. . . then I would move to a new planet.**

*or*

**. . . then I would move to in Kalamazoo.**

*or*

**. . . then I could ride it to the fair.**

*or*

**. . . then he would scratch the livelong day.**

Whoever provides the "then" also says the next "if."

A good game of "I Say 'If,' You Say 'Then'" can use real "if-then" combinations or become goofy. Enjoy the game and have a good laugh. If you want to make the game harder, you can limit the "if-then" combinations to real life. You can also limit the time you have to come up with the "then" answer. Try clapping three times between stating the "if," or count to ten. As you get better at the game, shorten the time between the "ifs" and "thens."

# THE THIGH BONE'S CONNECTED TO THE KNEE BONE

Have you ever seen a skeleton? Now, imagine a skeleton taken apart. It's just a pile of bones, right? Well . . . it's really more like a pile of puzzle pieces that go together in a special order.

## SKELETON DANCE

You can make your very own skeleton puppet and, once it's put together, you can make it dance!

**You'll need:**
scrap paper • a pencil • photocopy or tracing paper • white construction paper or lightweight white card stock • scissors • a black marker • paper clasps

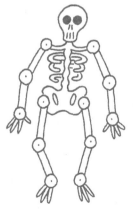

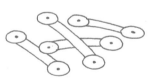

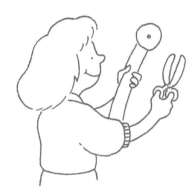

First, get some help to draw a skeleton on scrap paper. You might be able to copy or trace one from a book. Decide where the joints come together and mark them with a dot. Draw a circle around the dot.

Once you're happy with your drawing, ask if you can get it photocopied. If not, you can trace your drawing so you have two copies.

Then, cut out the pieces of your skeleton. Remember to leave the circle extensions at the joints so you can connect the pieces later. Next, use the cut out pieces like stencils and draw the skeleton on the white construction paper or card stock. Use a black marker to outline the pieces and cut them out.

Last, use paper clasps to connect the skeleton pieces at the joints. Then move your skeleton's limbs around and make it dance.

## MAKING PUZZLES

If you like putting puzzles together, you'll love making your own jigsaws.

**You'll need:**
**precut puzzle sheets or heavyweight card stock**
**• markers • a manila envelope**

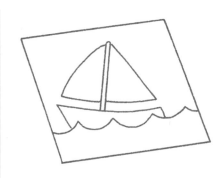

First, use markers to draw a colorful picture on precut puzzle sheets or card stock. You might want to draw a lovely scene or a picture of your favorite pet.

Next, take apart the puzzle pieces. If you've drawn your puzzle picture on card stock, draw lines to show how the puzzle should be cut into jigsaw-type pieces. Then get a grown-up to help you cut the puzzle apart. If you're used to doing puzzles with large pieces, cut large pieces. Don't make so many pieces that the puzzle is too hard to put back together.

Last, put together your very own puzzle. Invite your brothers, sisters, cousins, or friends to give it a try. When you're finished, store your puzzle in a manila envelope.

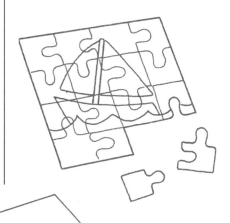

# DOMINOES

Dominoes are flat tiles or cards in the shape of a rectangle. Each rectangle is divided into two parts, or squares. On most dominoes, pips represent different numbers on each square. The pips resemble those on dice. In playing dominoes, you have to match a square already played with a new tile. By the time all the tiles are played, an interesting design is created.

## PICTURE DOMINOES

You can make your own set of dominoes.

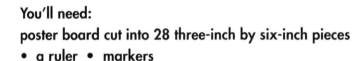

**You'll need:**
**poster board cut into 28 three-inch by six-inch pieces**
**• a ruler • markers**

First, draw a line down the middle of each piece of poster board to create the two domino faces.

## DRAW DOMINOES

A true set of dominoes includes all the combinations of numbers that can be shown by tossing two dice, plus all the numbers shown by throwing one die.

To play "Draw Dominoes," all the tiles are turned facedown and mixed. Each player draws one domino from the pile. The one who draws the tile with the most pips goes first. If you are using picture dominoes, you can decide which picture is most valuable, and so on, down to the blanks.

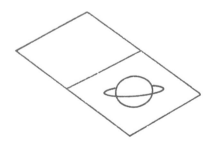

Then, think up six different drawings to use on your dominoes. You might choose a theme to help you, for example:

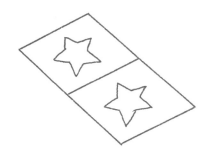

**toys**
　　　　　ball
　　　　　jump rope
　　　　　jacks
　　　　　top
　　　　　doll
　　　　　building block

**astronomy**
　　　　　star
　　　　　planet
　　　　　comet
　　　　　rocket
　　　　　galaxy
　　　　　moon

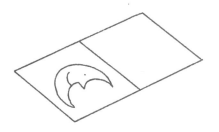

**animals**
　　　　　mammal
　　　　　bird
　　　　　lizard
　　　　　fish
　　　　　snake
　　　　　insect

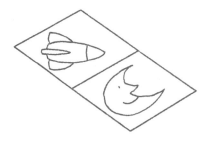

**weather**
　　　　　sunshine
　　　　　blue sky with clouds
　　　　　lightning
　　　　　rain
　　　　　snow
　　　　　rainbow

Then, all the players draw dominoes. If two or three people are playing, each player draws seven dominoes. If four people are playing, each player draws five dominoes.

Next, play begins. The first player places one domino in the center of the playing area. The next person has to match either side of the first player's domino. Dominoes can be laid down to create a straight line or can turn corners. If a domino has identical ends, it can be placed crosswise to create two open ends.

Next, use your marker to draw each type of picture on the dominoes. On some dominoes, you may want to draw the same picture twice. On others, draw a different picture. On still others, leave one face blank.

If you want to play dominoes according to the rules of the game, illustrate your picture dominoes according to the themes suggested on the previous page. If you need help, ask before you color the domino faces.

Now, you're ready for a game of picture dominoes.

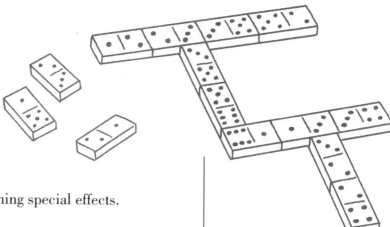

# DOMINO EFFECT

Use your domino tiles to build stunning special effects.

Set up your dominoes one by one on a narrow end. Place each domino about one inch apart. Snake the dominoes around or create spirals, waves, or block patterns.

Once all the dominoes are set up, gently tip the end domino into the domino next to it. Watch as the dominoes topple one by one.

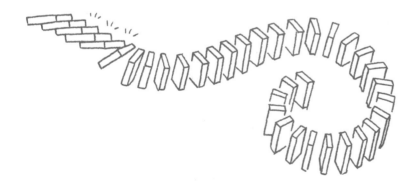

If a player doesn't have a domino that will fit on the open ends, he or she draws dominoes from the pile until a match can be made. If all the dominoes are drawn, the turn passes to the next player.

Play continues until one person plays all his or her dominoes.

Dominoes can also be played as a scoring game (see "Keeping Score," p. 118).

# THE ALPHABET SONG

A, *B, C, D, E, F, G* . . .

*H, I, J, K, L-M-N-O, P* . . .

*Q, R, S* . . .

*T, U, V* . . .

*W, X,*

*Y and Z*

*Now I know my ABCs.*

*Next time won't you sing with me.*

Once you know your letters (see Part Four: "Now I Know My ABC's"), you can play some games based on the alphabet.

## ALPHA-CLAPS

Play "Alpha-claps" with one friend—or a roomful. All you need to do is sing the alphabet song, but instead of singing all the letters, leave a few out. Clap your hands when you skip the letter.

**A, B, C, D, E, -CLAP-, G,**

and so on.

The players yell out the letter you clapped as you continue to sing the song.

Once you've mastered "Alpha-claps," try a more difficult version.

**You'll need:**
**scratch paper • pencils**

Pass out paper and pencils to everyone playing. Then choose a singer.

As the singer claps missing letters in the Alphabet Song, the players write down the missed letters. Ask an older person to referee your "Alpha-claps" rounds and see who gets the most claps correct.

## ALPHA-CARDS

Use a set of alphabet cards for this sequencing game. You can use the same cards for "Alphabet Soup" on page 82.

**You'll need:**
**alphabet cards • a brown paper sack**

Shuffle the alphabet cards and put them in the sack. Then, draw one alphabet card and place it on a table or open floor space. Then draw another card. Does it come before or after the first card? Decide where the card belongs and place it on the playing space.

Continue drawing alphabet cards and placing them in order until you've used all the cards. Test to see if you've placed them correctly by singing the alphabet song.

## ALPHA-PLAY

Stage an alphabet drama for your family and friends.

**You'll need:**
**4 to 5 people • alphabet cards**

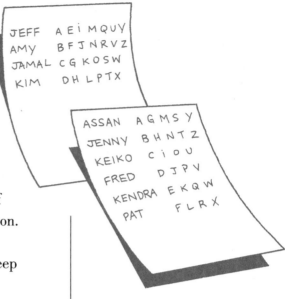

First, get together at least three friends who know the alphabet and the alphabet song.

Then, lay out alphabet cards in order. Decide the order of "characters," that is, who is going to be *A*, who *B*, and so on.

Next, figure out how to separate your alphabet cards to keep the drama going.

Next, have each character pick up his or her cards and hold them in order.

Last, as you sing the alphabet song, have each player run behind the other characters after his or her letter is sung to get into position for the next letter.

After a few rehearsals, you'll be ready for showtime!

# NOW I KNOW MY ABCs

## LETTERS AND SIMPLE WORDS

Letters and their sounds are introduced and practiced throughout the kindergarten year. Reinforce what your child learns in school by playing games that focus on letter recognition and phonics.

## 1. PICTURE THIS

These activities are designed to help your child learn the alphabet—both to recognize the letters and to pronounce them.

"Short Stop" focuses on vowel sounds. This will be difficult for many kindergartners. If it's too hard, save it. The activity is also appropriate for first graders and beyond. When practicing vowel sounds, focus on all long sounds or all short sounds. Don't mix long and short at first or your child may become confused and frustrated.

Alpha-picture cards can be purchased, but are fun to make with your child. Creating the cards may help your child better remember the lessons.

## 2. ALPHABET SOUP

Everyone has to eat—so why not eat alphabet soup? It's delicious, nutritious—and is one food your child should take free reign to play with!

Another recipe for learning letters is in "Clay Tablets." In addition to forming letters, your child can use clay to form simple words (although many kindergartners aren't ready for word recognition until the latter part of school year). You can also use clay tablets to spell out names—your child's, yours, or your pet's.

"Letter Box" let's your child show you—on an ongoing basis—what he or she is learning. Using "Letter Box" allows your child to have a special correspondence with you. It is a means of showing and communicating what he or she has learned. You may want to use "Letter Box" for other learning activities, too. For example, when your child learns to recognize numerals, numerals, too, can be put in the box.

## 3. MATCH GAME

These activities are geared to teach upper and lower case letters. Your child may call these capital and small letters.

Although these activities are fairly straightforward, they will be frustrating at best for a child who doesn't know the alphabet. Be sure your child has mastered the activities in "Picture This," and "Alphabet Soup" before attempting "Match Game."

## 4. THE SIGN SAYS . . .

Once your kindergartner has mastered the alphabet and can play the games in "Picture This" and "Alphabet Soup," introduce the activities in "The Sign Says…." These games are meant for kids on the move. They offer fun for everyone, as well as wonderful learning tools for early primary schoolers.

## 5. A, MY NAME IS ANNIE

Here is a set of activities for later in the kindergarten year. These games assume a sound knowledge of the alphabet and of letter sounds.

Introduce these activities by playing in teams. That means you and your kindergartner can work together. Once your kindergartner is playing along, you might want to bend the rules a bit, too. For example, make *j, q, x,* and *z* optional pass letters, or offer help on these difficult ones until your child commits a few combinations to memory.

## 6. TAG SALE

Much of reading is recognition. Word recognition comes from repeatedly seeing words. So why not offer your child the advantage of seeing simple words more often—many times each day, in fact. Set up a tag sale in your home and see how quickly your kindergartner is rattling off words.

Use the "Letter Box" for words, too. Your child can show you not only letters and numbers that he or she has learned, but also the vocabulary as it develops.

# PICTURE THIS

## VOWELS AND CONSONANTS

The letters of the alphabet are divided into two types: consonants and vowels.

**Vowels**

a

e

i

o

u

y (sometimes)

Use the picture alphabet to learn letters and their sounds. Remember, only the first sound of each word is the letter sound!

| | | | |
|---|---|---|---|
| short a | apple | ant | acrobat |
| long a | angel | apron | ace |
| b | bike | banjo | baseball |
| c | cake | computer | cap |
| d | dandelion | dog | devil |

**short e**

elephant      egg      engine

**long e**

ear      emu      eagle

**f**

fox      father      fruit

**hard g**

guitar      gate      goose

**soft g**

gem      gym      gypsy

**h**

horse      hippo      hand

**short i**

igloo      infant      inch

## Consonants

b
c
d
f
g
h
i
k
l
m
n
p
q
r
s
t
v
w
x
y
z

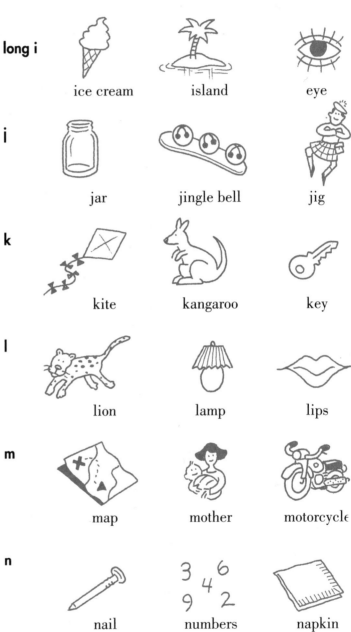

**long i**

ice cream    island    eye

**i**

jar    jingle bell    jig

**k**

kite    kangaroo    key

**l**

lion    lamp    lips

**m**

map    mother    motorcycle

**n**

nail    numbers    napkin

**short o**

octopus    olive    opera

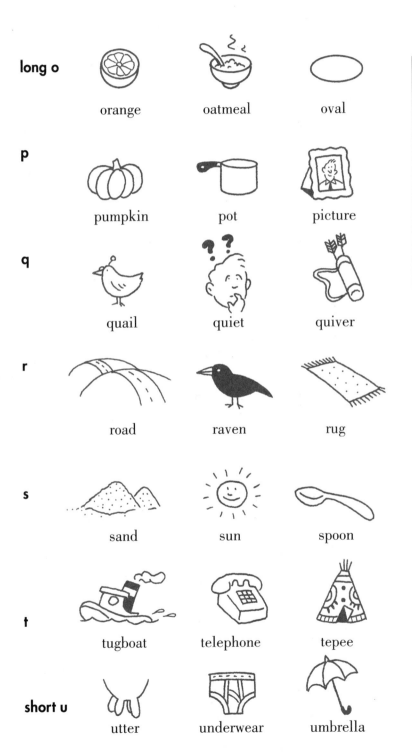

**long o**

orange     oatmeal     oval

**p**

pumpkin     pot     picture

**q**

quail     quiet     quiver

**r**

road     raven     rug

**s**

sand     sun     spoon

**t**

tugboat     telephone     tepee

**short u**

utter     underwear     umbrella

**long u**

ukulele    universe

**v**

vampire    violin    villain

**w**

watch    watermelon    walrus

**x**

xylophone

**y**

yak    yoyo    yard

**z**

zoo    zebra    zodiac

## SHORT STOP

Have you noticed how some letter sounds get mixed up with other letter sounds? Think of the sounds *a, e, i, o,* and *u*. Mix these sounds with the letter *b* sound. Together the *b* and the *a, e, i, o,* and *u* sounds work together to create words:

| | |
|---|---|
| **ba** | **bay** |
| **be** | **be** |
| **bi** | **buy** |
| **bo** | **bow** |
| **bu** | **boo** |

The letters *a, e, i, o, u,* and sometimes *y* mix with other letters to form sounds with meaning, or words.

## ALPHA-PICTURE CARDS

To make "Alpha-picture cards," follow the instructions for making alphabet cards (p. 70) but leave room to illustrate each letter. "Alpha-picture cards" can be used for all the same games as regular alphabet cards.

# ALPHABET SOUP

**M**mmmmm . . . delicious soup—and educational, too! Do you know the letters of the alphabet when you see them?

| | |
|---|---|
| A | N |
| B | O |
| C | P |
| D | Q |
| E | R |
| F | S |
| G | T |
| H | U |
| I | V |
| J | W |
| K | X |
| L | Y |
| M | Z |

The next time you have alphabet soup for lunch, ask if you can play with your food — just a little bit. If it's okay, give your soup a gentle swirl and try to find the letter *A*. Scoop it up with your spoon and eat it. Now look for the letter *B*. Continue through the alphabet until you've eaten all the letters.

# CLAY TABLETS

Use clay to make letters.

...............
: **You'll need:**
: **modeling clay or play dough**
...............

First, form several long snakes with the clay or play dough.

Next, take a few pieces of snake and form the letter *A*. Then, form *B*. Or make letters in any order you like. You can break off bits of snake to make crossbars on the letters.

When you're finished, you'll have a clay alphabet.

When you've learned a few words, use your clay letters to form words. You can also write words in clay tablets.

## ANCIENT WRITING

People who lived in ancient times didn't have pencils and paper to write with. Instead, they cut letters into stone or dug them into clay tablets.

You can pretend to be like the ancients. Press modeling clay into a flat tablet. Then, using a stick, write your letters in the soft clay.

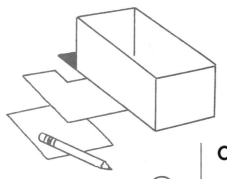

# COUNTRY-STYLE LETTER BOX

There are 26 letters in the alphabet. That's a lot of letters to learn. Instead of making the job of learning your letters a big one, why not make it a little easier. All you have to do is learn a letter or two each day. Once you've learned a letter, put it in a letter box.

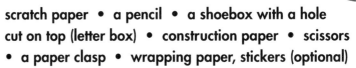

**You'll need:**
scratch paper • a pencil • a shoebox with a hole cut on top (letter box) • construction paper • scissors • a paper clasp • wrapping paper, stickers (optional)

First, make your letter box. Ask a grown-up to help you cut a hole in the top of a shoebox (or similarly sized box). Then cut a letter box "flag" out of construction paper and fasten it to your letter box. Assemble the box so it's ready to receive letters. The flag should be down. You may want to cover the outside of the box with wrapping paper or decorate it with stickers. Use your imagination.

Then, learn a letter and practice writing it on scratch paper. When you've got the letter down, write it once again on a clean sheet of scratch paper.

Next, fold the paper and slide it into the hole on top of your letter box. Be sure you turn the flag up so your folks know they've got a letter inside!

Last, see what response you get from the letter in the letter box. Maybe you'll get a letter back!

# MATCH GAME

L etters come in two forms—capital and small. The letters look like this:

| | |
|---|---|
| A | a |
| B | b |
| C | c |
| D | d |
| E | e |
| F | f |
| G | g |
| H | h |
| I | i |
| J | j |
| K | k |
| L | l |
| M | m |
| N | n |
| O | o |
| P | p |
| Q | q |
| R | r |
| S | s |
| T | t |
| U | u |
| V | v |
| W | w |
| X | x |
| Y | y |
| Z | z |

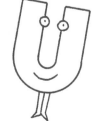

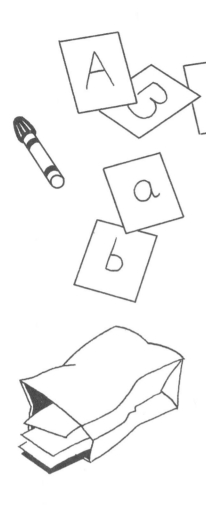

## LETTER MATCH

Now that you know what the letters look like, get ready to play "Letter Match."

**You'll need:**
52 index cards or pieces of construction paper, poster board, etc. • a marker • a paper sack

First, using a marker, copy one letter on each index card. When you're finished, you'll have a complete set of alphabet cards.

Then, put the alphabet cards in a paper sack and mix them up.

Next, pull out one card at a time and lay them faceup on a table, pairing off capital and small letters as you draw them.

If you and a friend have alphabet cards, you can have a race. See who can match capital and small letters faster!

## CONCENTRATION

Use your alphabet cards to play "Concentration," too.

First, lay out all your alphabet cards facedown on a playing area. Then turn over one card. Next, turn over a second card. If the cards match, pull them off the playing area. If they don't match, turn both cards facedown again and turn over another pair.

You can play "Concentration," with a friend. Both of you must try to remember where the letters are so you can turn over matches. If you both have cards, race to see who can pair off the deck first.

## WORD MATCH AND CONCENTRATION

Make "Letter Match" and "Concentration" new games by creating a set of word cards.

**You'll need:**
**20 or more index cards or construction paper, poster board, etc., cut into card size • a marker**

Once you know 20 or more words, copy them onto cards to make a deck of word cards. Use these cards the same way as you did for "Letter Match" and "Concentration."

# THE SIGN SAYS . . .

## LETTER HUNT

When you're driving in the car, play "Letter Hunt." When you're in the grocery store, play "Letter Hunt." When you're at a restaurant, play "Letter Hunt."

First, pick a letter. Then, look for the letter everywhere you go. If you're in the car, hunt for your letter on road signs. In the grocery store, hunt for your letter on packages, posters, and specials signs. Or look for your letter on a restaurant menu or in the articles and signs on the restaurant walls.

## SIGN GAME

Turn "Letter Hunt" into a contest. You can play with a friend or a family member—or with a whole group of people. The "Sign Game" is especially fun to play on car trips.

First, announce to everyone that the "Sign Game" has begun.

Then, have each person look for letters of the alphabet—in alphabetical order—on signs along the road. You have to find an *A* before you move on to *B*, and so forth. Also, you can't use another player's letters. The first player to spot a letter on a sign is the only player who can use that sign for the letter. The player who makes it through the alphabet first wins.

A tougher version of the "Sign Game" allows players to use only the first letters of words on signs. A still tougher version requires players to locate the letters and say the words they begin, as well.

Some letters are tough to find: *j*, *q*, *y*, and *z*. You might want to make special rules about those letters. For example, you could allow using license plates that begin with the tough letters. Or you may want to allow a "tough letter bank." That means you can spot tough letters no matter where you are in the alphabet and save them in the bank for when you need them.

# A, MY NAME IS ANNIE

## WHERE IN THE WORLD IS THAT?

**"A, My Name Is Annie" will introduce you to some new place-names. Or, you might want to use some funny-sounding names of real places.**

**Do you know where Timbuktu is? Or Oshkosh? How about Sri Lanka or even Kokomo? If your family has a book of maps or if you have the chance to use one at the library, ask for some help in finding the places you come across in playing "A, My Name Is Annie." And while you're looking through the pages of maps, you might locate a few extra place-names for your next round of play.**

## WORD EXCHANGE

Here's a chance to use your alphabet cards again (see "Match Game," p. 85). Or simply follow alphabetical order. You'll need a friend to play with—the more the merrier!

> **You'll need:**
> **alphabet cards • a paper sack (or alphabet cards in a shuffled deck)**

First, pick a card to see who goes first. The player who draws the letter closest to *A* goes first. Return all the alphabet cards to the paper bag or the deck and shuffle them. If you're not using alphabet cards, simply choose someone to start.

Then, the first player draws a card. He or she has to think of a word that begins with the letter on that card. For example:

| | |
|---|---|
| a | apple |
| b | balloon |
| c | cat |

Players are eliminated if they can't come up with a word for their letter or if the word they choose is not correct. For example, if a player draws *S* and says "circus," the player is out of the game.

The last player remaining wins the game.

## A, MY NAME IS ANNIE

Here's a variation on "Word Exchange" that includes names of
people, places, and things. To begin, the first player draws a
letter from a deck of alphabet cards or simply begins with *A*
(play will follow alphabetical order). Then the player states his
or her letter, saying, for example:

**A, my name is Annie.**
**I come from Alabama**
**And I'm bringing home some apples.**

The next player recites, for example:

**B, my name is Ben.**
**I come from Berlin**
**And I'm bringing home some bananas.**

This game might be a little tough at first, but after a while, you'll
remember combinations that work for each letter. You'll need at
least two people to play. It's a good idea to play with an older
person who knows how to spell fairly well and who knows some
geography, too.

Players are eliminated if they can't recite the combination.
The last player remaining in the game wins.

# TAG SALE

You probably know the names of all the types of furniture, appliances, and decorations in your house. But do you know what those words look like written out? If not, try "Tag Sale."

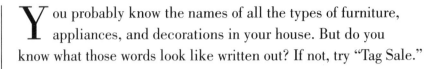

**You'll need:**
**adhesive-backed paper tags (or tags with string)**
• **a marker**

Ask your parents if you can set up a make-believe tag sale in your home. You can have your tag sale in your bedroom, or maybe the family room, bathroom, and kitchen, too.

First, get an older person to help you spell out the names of your home's furnishings. For example:

| | |
|---|---|
| bed | chair |
| couch | recliner |
| bookshelves | television |
| table | lamp |
| refrigerator | sink |
| bathtub | vanity |
| stairs | fireplace |
| cabinet | |

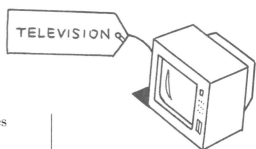

As an extra attraction, you might also want to label the names of the rooms:

**bedroom**
**living room**
**dining room**
**kitchen**
**family room**
**laundry room**
**bathroom**

Write down the names on the adhesive-backed notepaper or tags and stick or tie them in place.

To make a sale, ask a friend or family member to quiz you. "What letters spell bed?" you're asked. "B-E-D," you answer. When you can spell a word correctly, take down the tag.

# SOUNDS GOOD

## PHONICS AND WORD PLAY

Letter sounds are learned as preparation for reading. Learning the sounds is difficult for some kindergartners, and rather simple for others. Even children who've memorized the alphabet with ease can have a hard time recalling letter sounds.

Use the activities in this section to help your child learn letter sounds, and use it, too, to learn about your child's learning style. If your kindergartner seems to have difficulty with letter sounds, discuss your concerns with your kindergartner's teacher.

# 1. PUCKER UP AND TWIST YOUR TONGUE

"Monkey Say, Monkey Do" and "Alien Speak" familiarize your child with his or her sound-making abilities and give license for some fun sound play. The ability to recognize and repeat sounds is a fundamental reading skill. So let the chatter begin!

# 2. SOUND SCENES

This set of activities applies the skills in "Pucker Up and Twist Your Tongue" to identifying letter sounds in words. These activities will be difficult for many kindergartners, and may still be valuable to reinforce skills as your child enters first grade.

# 3. MORE THAN MOTHER GOOSE AND I SPY! NOW YOU TRY!

Rhyme is taught throughout the primary grades, but introduced through the poems and nursery verse you've read at bedtime from cradle days to the first day of kindergarten. If your child recognizes rhyme, he or she has developed a valuable reading tool.

In "More than Mother Goose," familiar rhymes are used to reinforce word recognition. As your child learns the rhymes, the words within the rhyming stanzas can be sorted and represented in pictures and words.

"I Spy! Now You Try!" provides more straightforward rhyming activities. Don't be surprised if your kindergartner falters now and then, confusing, for example, beginning sounds with the ending (rhyming) sounds.

# PUCKER UP AND TWIST YOUR TONGUE

Have you ever clicked your tongue or flapped your lips? You've probably done both and more to make funny sounds. And you've probably been making those sounds for years already!

Making funny mouth sounds is a great way to get your lips ready for reading out loud. In order to read, you have to understand that sounds are put together to make words. And in order to understand sounds, you have to know how they are made.

So keep puckering, clucking, whistling, and clacking. Think about the sounds you're making and how you're making them. Are you using your tongue? Your lips? Touch your neck and feel your vocal cords. Are they vibrating?

## MONKEY SAY, MONKEY DO

Your mom might go mad or your dog might go crazy, but you'll have a blast while everyone else goes bonkers.

**You'll need:**
a speaker to ape • a mirror (if you're playing alone)

If you're on your own, simply turn on a radio or television set. For monkey talk, even the dullest talk program is a good choice. Simply listen to the radio announcer. Then repeat a word or two that you hear. Repeat the word over and over again, more and more slowly.

Concentrate on each sound in the word. Be sure to move your facial position to make each separate sound in the word.

Now, look at yourself in the mirror. Your slow speech and movements might well remind you of a monkey!

If you're interested in some serious monkey business, get your friends to play "Monkey Say, Monkey Do." You can ape a word or phrase said on radio or television, or you and your friends can take turns suggesting words to imitate. You can share a mirror or simply look at your friends as you all repeat the chosen word. See how long you can last without laughing like a monkey!

## ALIEN SPEAK

If you like "Monkey Say, Monkey Do," you'll love "Alien Speak."

Imagine you've just landed on planet Earth. You have instantly learned the language of the earthlings, but, like aliens in the movies, you can only say the words in one tone and at one speed. Every sound in every word takes the same amount of time to say and no sounds are louder or softer than any other.

As you communicate with earthlings, listen to the individual sounds of the words you are saying. What position is your mouth in when you say "Mars" or "planet"? Do you use your lips to make the sounds? Your tongue?

# SOUND SCENES

## IN THE BEGINNING . . .

Look at the scenes pictured below. Name the things you see in them. You'll find letters from the alphabet in, or next to, many of the items in the pictures. The sounds made by these letters are the same as the beginning sounds in the names of the items.

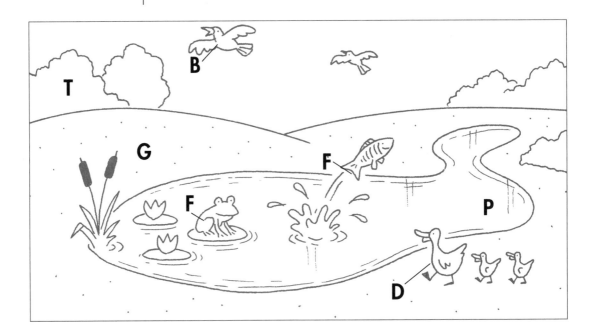

## FINISH LINE

Now, look at the same scene again. What's different? Nothing—except this time the letters in, or next to, the items stand for the sounds that you hear at the end of the words.

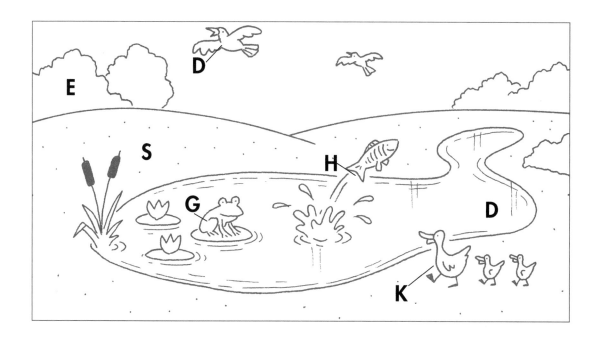

## MEET ME IN THE MIDDLE

Look at the pictures below. Each panel shows words that have
the same beginning and ending sound, but different sounds in the
middle. Say each word out loud. Then, eliminate the beginning
sound and the ending sound. What's left? The sound in the
middle, of course!

b _ t

d _ g

t _ n

c _ t

f _ g

b _ n

h _ g

f _ n

s _ d

## POET- CORNER

Sometimes letter sounds are also word sounds. If you know your letter sounds, you might be able to read some of the poems below.

O, M-L-E,
What X-T-C
I always feel
When U I C.


Who R U?
Y R U here?
Could U B A visitor
Who's unexpected here?

# MORE THAN MOTHER GOOSE

## PICTURE RHYMES

You've probably heard quite a few nursery rhymes. Some are so familiar you can probably recite them. But if you saw them printed on a page, could you read them?

Take a look at the following picture clues to old favorites. Then look at the picture rhymes. Now, can you also read nursery rhymes?

## PICTURE CLUES:

Hey, diddle, diddle,

The [cat] and the [fiddle],

The [cow] jumped over the [moon];

The little [dog] laughed

To see such sport,

And the [dish] ran away with the [spoon].

## THE REAL MOTHER GOOSE

Have you ever wondered if there was a real Mother Goose? Her name has been recognized by children around the world for hundreds of years.

No one knows for sure if there really was a Mother Goose. However, some believe the name came from Goose-Footed Bertha, the mother of the emperor Charlemagne, who lived in France more than 1,200 years ago. Goose-Footed Bertha was famous for her storytelling.

Others believe Mother Goose was the mother-in-law of a Boston printer named Thomas Fleet. According to legend, he published in about 1719 a collection of children's stories by his dear Mistress Goose.

# PICTURE CLUES:

Little

Sat on a  ,

Eating her

Along came a  ,

Who sat down beside her

And frightened  away.

# PICTURE CLUES:

There was an  who lived in a  ,

She had so many she didn't know what to do;

She gave them some without any

And she kissed them all soundly and put them to

## PICTURE CLUES:

Went up the

To fetch a  of water;

 fell down,

And broke his crown,

And  came tumbling after.

## PICTURE CLUES:

Rock-a-bye, [baby], on the [tree],

When the [wind] blows the [cradle] will rock;

When the bough breaks, the [cradle] will fall,

And down will come [baby], [cradle] and all.

We know for certain that John Newbery, who lived in London, published a collection of nursery rhymes in 1781. He called his collection Mother Goose's Melody. Newbery's book was printed in the United States in 1785.

So was there ever a real Mother Goose? We'll never know for sure—except to say that there's a bit of Mother Goose in everyone.

## RHYME THIEF

You are the rhyme thief—but you've left a few clues behind.
Create your own picture clues for nursery rhymes and see if your
family and friends can solve the case of the missing rhymes.

**You'll need:**
**paper • a pencil • crayons or markers (optional)**

First, think of a nursery rhyme. Look in one of your favorite
books for ideas.

Then, on one sheet of paper, draw pictures of the characters or
the things in one rhyme. Be sure to use a separate sheet of paper
(or a separate part of a sheet) for each rhyme or your clues may
become confused.

Next, test the rhyme detectives in your home.
Ask your family if they can solve
the case of the missing rhymes.

# I SPY! NOW, YOU TRY!

## RHYME STRINGS

Make a "Rhyme String." You don't need thread or rope. You won't have to spin straw or tie twine. That's because a rhyme string isn't a string that you can see. You can't sew with it or tie packages.

To make a "Rhyme String," you need a mouth and an imagination. All you have to do is pick a word and then say as many rhyming words—real or made up—that you can think of. The more rhymes you make, the longer your rhyme string.

| laugh | or | spring |
|-------|-----|--------|
| calf | | nothing |
| staff | | cling |
| giraffe | | brrrring |
| plaff | | something |
| graff | | sting |
| zigglezaff | | fling |
| | | gring |
| | | bring |

string
thing
nothing
sting
gring
bring
cling

## DR. SEUSS

Dr. Seuss was a master at making up rhymes. In his books, you meet such creations as a Tufted Mazzurka from the Island of Yerka and Brown Barba-loots who eat Truffula Fruits, not to mention a Cat in the Hat and a turtle named Yertle.

Dr. Seuss was born in 1904 in Springfield, Massachusetts. He worked as an advertising artist, using his real name—Theodor Seuss Geisel. At first, he wrote and illustrated children's books as a hobby. When his book *And to Think That I Saw It on Mulberry Street* was published in 1937, it carried the author name "Dr. Seuss." Like Dr. Seuss books, the Dr. Seuss name is also a famous creation!

Dr. Seuss has delighted generations of children throughout the world with his witty, colorful, and thoughtful stories. Although his books live on, the gifted rhymer died in 1991.

## LEWIS CARROLL

Lewis Carroll was a master of reinventing existing poems. His poem "Father William" is now a well-remembered favorite that Carroll wrote to imitate a popular poem of his day.

Lewis Carroll, who was born in England in 1832, was also a master of made-up words and imaginary places. One of Carroll's best-loved poems, "Jabberwocky," is a classic nonsense poem from which comes the word chortle, to sing or chant with glee. "Chortle" was so descriptive that the nonsense word was accepted into standard English!

# RHYME STRING FOR TWO (OR MORE)

Why not make rhyme strings with a friend, or with two, three, or four friends? All you have to do is take turns thinking up rhyming words.

# INVENT-A-RHYME

Play a little "Invent-a Rhyme." Discover the poet within you. All you have to do is fill in the blanks with rhyming words.

I went to the park _today_
With two of my friends to _play_.
We had lots of _fun_
And when it was _done_
We were all feeling happy and _gay_!

The night was stormy,
The lights went _out_.
I was much too frightened
To scream or _shout_.

Instead I trembled
And hid my _head_
Beneath the covers
On my _bed_.

Homer Bassett is a ___dog___
Whose body looks like a furry ___log___ .
His ears are long, his paws are ___wide___ .
He's odd, but he's my joy and ___pride___ .

You can use your favorite poems to play "Invent-a Rhyme." Simply come up with new endings to the rhyming lines. Don't worry if your first few efforts don't make sense. It's fun just to create the rhyme. But you might surprise yourself and come up with a brilliant new version of an old standard poem.

Like so many of his words and characters, Lewis Carroll's name was also made up. Carroll's real name was Charles Lutwidge Dodgson (see also Dr. Seuss, p. 105). A mathematics professor at Oxford University in England, Dodgson was inspired by Alice Lidell, a child and friend, to write children's stories. Alice was married and had moved from Oxford when Carroll finally gave up teaching in 1872 to focus on writing. By this time, he had already published his Alice stories, *Alice's Adventures in Wonderland* and *Through the Looking-Glass.* Carroll died in Guildford, England, in 1898.

# COUNT ON IT

## NUMBERS AND COUNTING

The skills involved in recognizing numbers are essentially the same as those used in recognizing letters. Counting is a sequence skill. Like these other learning skills, number recognition and counting comes easily to some and harder to others.

Although your child may not be proficient at numbers and counting going in to the kindergarten year, your child should have a fair mastery of the numerals 1 to 20 and be able to count in order from 1 to 20. The following activities will help your child develop these skills—and help you evaluate your child's progress along the way.

## 1. THE NUMBERS GAME

Your kindergartner may not be able to count reliably at the beginning of the school year, but many kindergartners will master counting to 20 and beyond before entering first grade. Here are a set of activities to help learn and reinforce counting skills. Continue to play these games over the months and, perhaps, years. Make them more challenging simply by adding more numbers to the counting sequence. Establish a goal of 10, then 20, then 100. Once your child is comfortable, press on to 1,000 as a new goal, and so on.

## 2. ONE MORE, PLEASE!

Basic addition is introduced in most kindergarten classes. If your child is confident in his or her counting, use these activities to explain simple addition. After all, counting is really addition by 1s.

## 3. KEEPING SCORE

By the end of the school year, most kindergartners can count up to 20. Some grasp basic addition. In order to keep score, a child must possess both skills. Consequently, this set of scoring activities are too difficult for many kindergartners. They're included here for parents whose children are ready for these math challenges.

## 4. WHO CAME IN FIRST

Ordinal numbers are introduced as an alternate way of counting. Many children relate to ordinals in the context of prizes, so that's how they're treated in the activities here.

## 5. WHAT DAY IS IT, ANYWAY?

Time is a very difficult concept for young children to grasp. Time is taught throughout the early primary years. Rare is the child who can truly tell time in the kindergarten year—but introduce the ideas to your kindergartner and continue to build on them over the first and second grade years.

## 6. CASH IN

Like time, money is difficult for many children to understand. But most kindergartners are familiar with pennies, nickels, and dimes by year's end.

Use the activities in "Cash In" as much for counting practice as to explain value. The former is fundamental, the latter very challenging for a young mind.

# THE NUMBERS GAME

## COUNTING TO 10

Use the pictures below to help you count to 10.

| 1 | one | 🐌 |
| 2 | two | ☆ ☆ |
| 3 | three | 🐟 🐟 🐟 |
| 4 | four | ○ ○ ○ ○ |
| 5 | five | 🌼 🌼 🌼 🌼 🌼 |
| 6 | six | □ □ □ □ □ □ |
| 7 | seven | 🐦 🐦 🐦 🐦 🐦 🐦 🐦 |
| 8 | eight | △ △ △ △ △ △ △ △ |
| 9 | nine | 🌳 🌳 🌳 🌳 🌳 🌳 🌳 🌳 🌳 |
| 10 | ten | 🕷 🕷 🕷 🕷 🕷 🕷 🕷 🕷 🕷 🕷 |

## NUMBER CARDS

Make a set of picture cards and use them to play counting games.

> **You'll need:**
> 20 index cards or pieces of poster board • markers

Write each of the numbers 1 through 10 on a separate index card.

## GO FISH

A favorite children's card game is *Go Fish*. Do you know how to play?

Using a standard deck of playing cards, deal seven cards to each player. Pair any matching cards in your hand and turn the pair upside down on the playing area.

The person to the left of the dealer starts by asking the next player (to the left) for a card to match one already in his or her hand.

Next, draw pictures to show the quantities one through ten on the remaining index cards. You can copy the pictures and numbers shown above or make up your own pictures. Copy the words for the numbers on both sets of cards. Now, you're ready for some games.

## NUMBER PAIRS

"Number Pairs" is a numbers version of "Match Game" (p. 85).

**You'll need:**
**number cards • a paper sack**

First, put the number cards in the paper sack and mix them up.

Then, draw out one card and place it face up on the playing area.

Next, draw another card. If it matches the first card, pair them off and put them aside. If the card has no match, place it face up on the playing area.

Draw and pair all the number cards until they're paired off.

You can play "Number Pairs" with your friends. All you'll need is two sets of number cards. Whoever can pair off their set fastest wins the game.

If the next player has the card, he or she must give it up. The asker then pairs off the match, puts it facedown on the table, and asks for another match. When the next player cannot provide the asker with a match, he or she says, "Go fish." Then the asker draws one card from the deck and the play moves to the next person. The next player becomes the asker. The game ends when a player has paired off an entire hand and is holding no more cards. Then all players count the number of pairs they've made. The player with the most pairs wins.

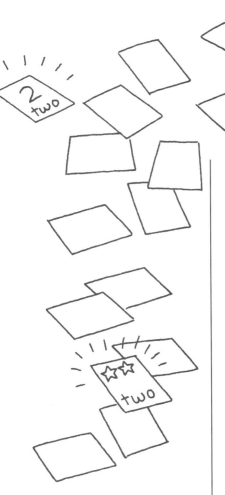

## NUMBER CONCENTRATION

Use your number cards to play "Number Concentration." First, lay out all your number cards facedown on a playing area. Then, turn over one card. Next, turn over a second card. If the cards match, pull them off the playing area. If they don't match, turn both cards facedown again and turn over another pair.

## COUNTING TO 20

Once you've mastered counting to 10, work your way up to 20. Take a look at the pictures below. They'll help you count from 11 to 20.

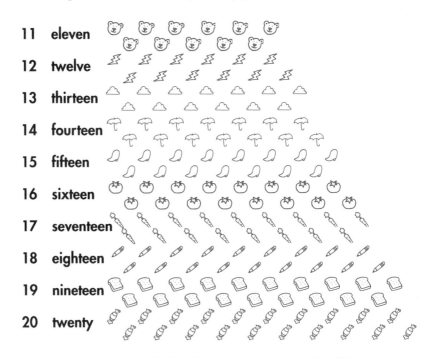

| 11 | eleven |
| 12 | twelve |
| 13 | thirteen |
| 14 | fourteen |
| 15 | fifteen |
| 16 | sixteen |
| 17 | seventeen |
| 18 | eighteen |
| 19 | nineteen |
| 20 | twenty |

You can make number cards for 11 through 20, too. You'll have twice as many cards as before, so "Number Pairs" and "Number Concentration" will be twice as challenging!

# ONE MORE, PLEASE!

Have you ever asked for seconds after eating something really delicious? Have you ever asked for thirds?

Have you ever asked for seconds twice?

Seconds twice is really thirds, right?

Let's look at how the numbers work.

|  |  |
|---|---|
| 1 | 5 + 1 = 6 |
| 1 + 1 = 2 | 6 + 1 = 7 |
| 2 + 1 = 3 | 7 + 1 = 8 |
| 3 + 1 = 4 | 8 + 1 = 9 |
| 4 + 1 = 5 | 9 + 1 = 10 |

"I GAVE HIM SECONDS."

"NO, I GAVE HIM SECONDS."

## PLUS SIGN AND EQUAL SIGN

**Do you know what this sign means?**

**It's the plus sign and it means and, add to, or plus.**

**When you use numbers, + means to put numbers together, or add.**

**1 + 1**

**Do you know what this sign means?**

**It's the equal sign, and it means is equal to or the same as.**

**So, when you have**

**it is equal to**

**2**

**or**

## 1 + 1 = 2

# PILES OF PENNIES

Watch your money grow!

**You'll need:**
**56 pennies (or paperclips, hair pins, washers, marbles, etc.)**

First, divide the pennies into piles. Put one penny in the first pile, two in the second, three in the third, and so on, until you have ten piles. You should have one penny left over.

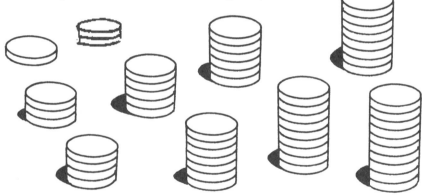

Now, take the extra penny and put it with the pile of one penny. Then, find the pile with the same number of pennies. It's the pile with two pennies.

Continue adding the extra penny to the other piles. What happens to the number of pennies in each pile? The number increases by one.

What do you suppose would happen if you added two pennies to each pile? Try it and see.

# NUMBER SENTENCES

You can write "Number Sentences" to describe "Piles of Pennies." Here's how you do it.

When you connect numbers using the **+** and **=** signs, you've made a number sentence. In fact, you've made a special kind of number sentence called an addition sentence.

# NUMBER JUNGLE

Find your way through the "Number Jungle."

You'll need:
number cards

First, shuffle your deck of number cards.

Then, lay the cards out in a line.

Next, sort the cards in their correct order: 1, 2, 3, 4, and so on up to 10 or 20.

When you've finished, you'll have succcessfully made it through the "Number Jungle."

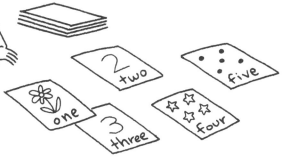

# KEEPING SCORE

If you can add 1 + 1, and so on, you can keep score. You can make some of the games in this book more exciting with a little scorekeeping. For example, look at "Carnival Coin Toss" on page 46. The scorekeeping is kind of complicated. But if you start out with some simpler scorekeeping, you'll be keeping track of "Coin Toss," too, in no time at all.

## SIMPLE SCORING

For many games, such as "Concentration"(p. 86), "Match Game" (p. 85), and "Number Pairs" (113), you may want to play more than one round. Then you can determine the winner and grand champion at the end of several games by keeping track of who has won the most.

A simple way to keep a game score is to use tally markers. Here's what they look like:

Ⅲ̶Ⅱ

Here's how you use them:

Ⅲ̶Ⅱ    Ⅲ̶Ⅱ    Ⅲ̶Ⅱ

Tally marks are always grouped by five. That means you draw four tally marks and cross through them with the fifth mark. If Bob has won seven games and you have won three, your tally sheet would look like the picture at left.

## ADDING THE SCORE

Remember "Dominoes?" The game is described on page 64. How about "Carnival Coin Toss" on page 46? In order to score these games, you can take a shortcut by simply adding the numerals. Or you can use your tally markers until you're more comfortable adding numerals.

Here's how to do it.

## SCORING COIN TOSS

Translate scores into tally marks.

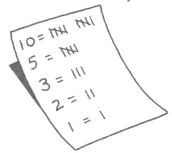

Then count up the tally marks.

## SCORING DRAW DOMINOES

To score "Draw Dominoes," players add up the total number of pips left on their unused dominoes. Then all the players' pip totals are added together to get a score. The winner of the round—that is, the player who runs out of dominoes first—gets this score on the scoresheet. Play continues until one player gets 100 or more points on the scoresheet.

So how do you score "Draw Dominoes" without adding numerals?
The same way you did for "Coin Toss." Here's a hint, though.
It takes 20 tally sets to equal 100.

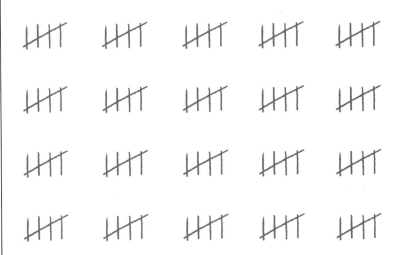

The winner at "Draw Dominoes" will be the first to get this many
tally marks!

# WHO CAME IN FIRST?

"I was here first."

"I was second."

"Jenny came in third, but Rick was sixth."

You know the counting numbers. They're 1, 2, 3, 4, 5 . . . and they are called "one, two, three, four, five . . . ." Sometimes numbers are used to tell the order in which something happens. Numbers that tell order are not counting numbers, but ordinal numbers. The ordinal numbers up to ten are called:

**first
second
third
fourth
fifth
sixth
seventh
eighth
ninth
tenth**

## BLUE RIBBON WINNERS

If you want to make your prize ribbons really authentic, use traditional colors.

For the ribbons, use:

blue for first place
red for second place
white for third place

For the burst stickers, use:

gold for first place
silver for second place
bronze for third place

Sometimes they are written this way:

1st
2nd
3rd
4th
5th
6th
7th
8th
9th
10th

## PRIZE PATROL

Ever enter a contest and win a prize? Did you win first prize or second prize?

Maybe you won third prize.

It's fun to win prizes. It's also fun to make up prizes—and award prize ribbons.

**You'll need:**
ribbon cut into 5-inch pieces • string or thin ribbon
cut and tied into loops • 2-inch burst stickers in gold,
silver, and bronze or paper cut into cut into 2-inch
diameter circles • pen or stylus

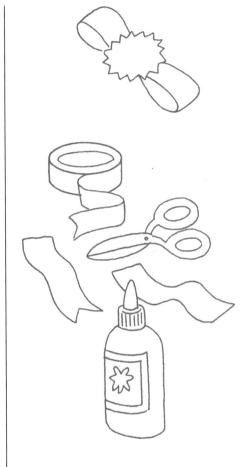

First, press a burst sticker over two pieces of ribbon.

Then, place a loop on the sticker so that it hangs off the top of the
seal, that is, off the opposite end of the seal from the ribbon ends.

Next, press a second burst sticker on the back to secure the
ribbons and loop.

If you are using paper cut into circles, glue the ribbons
and loop onto one circle, then glue the second circle
to the first, securing the ribbons and loop in between.

Last, write the prize number on your handmade awards
and pass them out to all the winners you know!

# WHAT DAY IS IT, ANYWAY?

O n sunny days when you're outside playing with friends, building forts, riding bikes, swimming, running, jumping— the day passes much too quickly.

On rainy days when your parents are busy and your sister won't play with you or your brother is at someone else's house for a birthday party and none of your friends are free to come over— the day passes much too slowly.

You may find it hard to believe, but rainy days pass just as quickly as sunny days. The same is true the other way around. Sunny days pass just as slowly as rainy days. In fact, each and every day is 24 hours long—not a moment shorter or longer!

People are constantly measuring time. School starts at nine o'clock, bedtime is at eight, you go to the dentist at four, your favorite television program is at six.

When you're in kindergarten, older people usually keep track of time for you. But you can measure it, too, using familiar objects in your home.

# CALENDAR

The calendar measures the days, weeks, and months in a year.
There are seven days in each week. The days are called:

**Sunday**
**Monday**
**Tuesday**
**Wednesday**
**Thursday**
**Friday**
**Saturday**

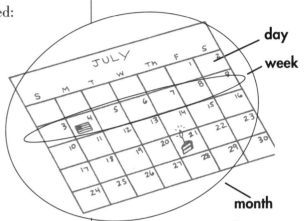

Each month is made up of about four weeks. The weeks do not
have special names.

Each year is made up of twelve months. The months are called:

**January**
**February**
**March**
**April**
**May**
**June**
**July**
**August**
**September**
**October**
**November**
**December**

Make a calendar of your own. Mount it where you can reach it. You can tick off the days and months and measure time between favorite events!

Think about the fun things that you do in a particular month. For example, you might go to summer camp in August, or visit a relative in February. In which month do you celebrate your birthday? Don't forget the holidays.

## CLOCKS

Clocks are also used to measure time. They measure the minutes and hours in each day. There are 60 minutes in each hour, and 24 hours in each day.

You've probably got a clock or two in your home, and they probably look like this:

or this:

The little hand on the clock tells you what hour it is, for example, one o'clock, four o'clock, and so on.

The digital clock tells time without using "hands." It tells the hour first, then the minutes, separating the two numbers with a colon (:).

You can make a practice clock with an hour hand (shorter arrow) and a minute hand (longer arrow).

**You'll need:**
a paper plate • a marker • a paper clasp

First, use the marker to write the numbers 1 through 12 on the paper plate. This will be the face of your clock. Be sure that the 12 is opposite the 6, and the 3 is opposite the 9.

Next, cut arrows out of the other sheet of construction paper. Make sure they are shorter than the distance from the middle of the construction paper circle to the numbers. One arrow should be slightly longer than the other.

Last, fasten the arrows to the circle with the paper clasp. The arrows will move freely around your clock face. Position the longer hand on the 12. This is the minute hand and you won't need to move this on your "hour clock."

Ask a grown-up to use the clock with you. For example, if you want to go outside to play, ask what time you need to come home. Then have the grown-up show you the time on the clock rather than tell you.

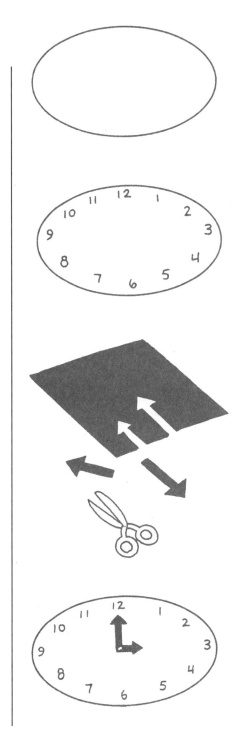

# CASH IN

## KNOW YOUR COINS

Look at the pictures of coins below. Do you know what the coins are called?

Do you know what they're worth? The coins below match their names and the number of cents each one represents.

| 1¢ | 5¢ | 10¢ | 25¢ |
| penny | nickel | dime | quarter |

## SWAP MEET

Ask an older person to play with you. See how many pennies you can get for other coins.

**You'll need:**
**100 pennies • 10 dimes • 20 nickels**

First, have the older person take the pennies. You take the rest of the change.

Then, offer a coin in exchange for pennies. Be sure to say the name of the coin. As you learn the value of the coin, also announce how many pennies you expect in exchange. For example:

**Here's a dime. May I please have 10 pennies?**

Once you've mastered "Swap Meet," you'll be ready for "Super Tag Sale."

## SUPER TAG SALE

> **You'll need:**
> several pennies (or assorted change) • Tag Sale set up (p. 92)

Take "Tag Sale" a step further and put a price on everything for sale!

First, decide how much items should cost and write the price on the tag sale labels.

Next, let the sale begin. Your friends or family members offer you the pennies in return for the labels on the tag sale items. Count carefully!

If you want to make the game more difficult, use dimes and nickels in addition to pennies.

## THE SYMBOL FOR CENTS

The symbol the means "cents" is ¢. So, if something costs one cent, it is written 1¢. The same symbol is used for something worth a nickel. Since a nickel is worth five cents, the cents sign follows the number five, or 5¢. So how much is a dime worth?

penny = 1 ¢
nickel = 5 ¢
dime = 10 ¢

# GOOD BOOKS TO READ

Aardema, Verna, illustrated by Leo and Diane Dillon. *Why Mosquitoes Buzz in People's Ears: A West African Tale.* (New York: Dial Press, 1975).

Anderson, Hans Christian, illustrated by Robert Van Nutt. *The Ugly Duckling.* (New York: Scroll Press, 1971).

Anno, Mitusumasa. *Anno's Alphabet: An Adventure In Imagination.* (New York: Crowell, 1974).

Baker, Olaf, illustrated by Stephen Gammell. *Where The Buffaloes Begin.* (New York: F. Warne, 1981).

Bang, Molly. *Ten, Nine, Eight.* (New York: Greenwillow Books, 1983).

Barrett, Judith, illustrated by Ron Barrett. *Cloudy With A Chance Of Meatballs.* (New York: Atheneum, 1978).

Barton, Byron. *I Want To Be An Astronaut.* (New York: Crowell, 1988).

Bemelmans, Ludwig. *Madeline.* (New York: Viking Press, 1967).

Brown, Marcia. *Once A Mouse.* (New York: Scribner, 1961).

Burningham, John. *Mr. Gumpy's Outing.* (New York: Holt, Rinehart & Winston, 1970).

Burton, Virginia Lee. *The Little House.* (Boston: Houghton Mifflin, 1969).

Cendrars, Blaise, illustrated by Marcia Brown. *Shadow.* (New York: Scribner's, 1982).

Crews, Donald. *Freight Train.* (New York: Greenwillow Books, 1978).

dePaola, Tomie. *Strega Nona.* (Englewood Cliffs, N.J.: Prentice-Hall, 1975).

de Regniers, Beatrice Schenk, illustrated by Beni Montresor. *May I Bring A Friend?* (Weston, CT: Weston Woods, 1973).

Eichenberg, Fritz. *Ape In A Cape: An Alphabet Of Odd Animals.* (New York: Harcourt, Brace, 1952).

Emberley, Barbara, illustrated by Ed Emberley. *Drummer Hoff.* (Englewood Cliffs, N.J.: Prentice Hall, 1967).

Farjeon, Eleanor, illustrated by Edward Ardizzone. *The Little Bookroom.* (New York: H.Z. Walck, 1956).

Gag, Wanda. *Millions Of Cats.* (New York: Coward, McCann & Geoghegan, 1928).

Geisert, Arthur. *Pigs From A To Z.* (Boston: Houghton Mifflin, 1986).

Gerrard, Roy. *Sir Cedric.* (New York: Farrar Straus Giroux, 1984).

Gerstein, Mordicai. *The Mountains Of Tibet.* (New York: Harper & Row, 1987).

Goble, Paul. *The Girl Who Loved Wild Horses.* (Scarsdale, New York: Bradbury Press, 1978).

Goffstein, M.B. *An Artist.* (New York: Harper & Row, 1987).

Grifalconi, Ann. *The Village Of Round and Square Houses.* (Boston: Little Brown, 1986).

Grimm, Brothers, illustrated by Trina Schart Hyman. *Little Red Riding Hood.* (Orchard, Watts, 1987).

Haley, Gail E. *A Story, A Story.* (New York: Atheneum, 1970).

Hall, Donald, illustrated by Barbara Cooney. *Ox-Cart Man.* (New York: Viking Press,1979).

Hodges, Margaret and Trina Schart Hyman. *St. George and The Dragon.* (Boston: Little, Brown, 1984).

Hogrogian, Nonny. *One Fine Day.* (New York: Macmillan, 1971).

Hutton, Warwick. *Jonah and The Great Fish.* (New York: Crowell, 1970).

Joslin, Sesyle, illustrated by Maurice Sendak. *What Do You Say, Dear? What Do You Do, Dear?* (Mass: Addison-Wesley, 1958).

Jukes, Mavis, illustrated by Lloyd Bloom. *Like Jake And Me.* (New York, New York: Knopf: Random House, 1984).

Keats, Ezra Jack. *The Snowy Day.* (Harmonesworth, New York: Puffin Books, 1962).

Keizaburo, Tejima. *Swan Sky.* (New York: Philomel Books, 1983).

Khalsa, Dayal Kaur. *How Pizza Came To Queens.* (New York: C.N. Potter Publisher; Crown, 1989).

Kimmel, Eric, illustrated by Trina Schart Hyman. *Hershel And The Hanukkah Goblins.* (New York: Holiday House, 1989).

Krauss, Ruth, illustrated by Maurice Sendak. *A Hole Is To Dig: A First Book Of Definitions.* (New York: Harper, 1952).

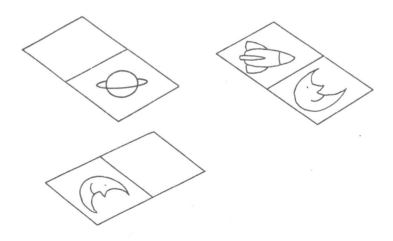

Kurelek, William. *A Prairie Boy's Winter.* (Boston: Houghton-Mifflin, 1973).

Lamorisse, Albert. *The Red Balloon.* (Garden City, N.Y.: Doubleday, 1957).

Langstaff, John, illustrated by Feodor Rojankovsky. *Frog Went A-Courtin'.* (New York: Harcourt & Brace, 1955).

Lasker, Joe. *Merry Ever After: The Story Of Two Medieval Weddings.* (New York: Viking Press, 1976).

Leodhas, Sorche Nic, illustrated by Nonny Hogrogian. *Always Room For One More.* (New York: Holt, Rinehart and Winston, 1965).

Lesser, Rika, illustrated by Paul O. Zelinsky. *Hansel and Gretel.* (New York: McGraw-Hill, 1982).

Lionni, Leo. *Frederick.* (New York: Pantheon, 1967).

Lionni, Leo. *Swimmy.* (New York: Pantheon, 1963).

Lobel, Arnold, illustrated by Anita Lobel. *On Market Street.* (New York: Greenwillow Books, 1981).

Lobel, Arnold. *Fables.* (New York: Harper & Row, 1980).

Locker, Thomas. *Where the River Begins.* (New York: Dial Books, 1984).

Low, Joseph. *Mice Twice.* (New York: Atheneum, 1980).

MacDonald, Suse. *Alphabatics.* (New York: Bradbury Press, 1986).

Mahy, Margaret, illustrated by Patricia McCarthy. *17 Kings And 42 Elephants.* (New York: Dial Books for Young Readers, 1987).

Marshall, James. *George and Martha.* (Boston: Houghton Mifflin, 1988).

McCloskey, Robert. *Make Way For Ducklings.* (New York: Viking Press, 1969).

McCloskey, Robert. *Blueberries For Sal.* (Weston, CT: Weston Woods Studio).

McDermott, Gerald. *Anansi The Spider: A Tale From The Ashanti.* (New York: Holt, Rinehart & Winston, 1972).

McKissick, Patricia C. *Mirandy And Brother Wind.* (New York: Knopf, 1988).

Mikolaycak, Charles. *Babushka: An Old Russian Folktale.* (New York: Holiday House, 1984).

Miles, Miska, illustrated by Peter Parnell. *Annie And The Old One.* (Boston: Little, Brown, 1971).

Mordvinoff, Will and Nicholas. *Finders Keepers.* (New York: McGraw-Hill, 1989).

Munro, Roxie. *The Inside-Outside Book Of New York City*. (New York: Dodd, Mead, 1985).

Musgrove, Margaret, illustrated by Leo and Diane Dillon. *Ashanti to Zulu: African Traditions*. (New York: Dial Press, 1976).

Paterson, Katherine, illustrated by Leo and Diane Dillon. *The Tale of The Mandarin Ducks*. (New York: Lodestar Books, 1990).

Pene Du Bois, William. *The Twenty-One Balloons*. (New York: Viking, 1947).

Perrault, Charles, illustrated by Fred Marcellio. *Puss In Boots*. (New York: Farrar Strauss Giroux, 1990).

Politi, Leo. *Song Of The Swallows*. (New York: C. Scribner's Sons, 1949).

Provensen, Alice and Martin. *The Glorious Flight: Across The Channel With Louis Bleriot*. (New York: Viking Press, 1983).

Ransome, Arthur, illustrated by Uri Shulevitz. *The Fool Of The World And The Flying Ship*. (New York: Farrar, Strauss and Giroux, 1968).

Raskin, Ellen. *Nothing Ever Happens On My Block.* (New York: Atheneum, 1966).

Ryan, Cheli Duran, illustrated by Arnold Lobel. *Hildilid's Night.* (New York: Macmillan, 1971).

Rylant, Cynthia, illustrated by Stephen Gammell. *The Relatives Came.* (New York: Bradbury Press, 1985).

San Souci, Robert D., illustrated by Jerry Pinkney. *The Talking Eggs: A Folktale From The American South.* (New York: Dial Books for Young Readers,1989).

Segal, Lore, illustrated by Paul O. Zelinsky. *The Story Of Mrs. Lovewright and Purrless Her Cat.* (New York: Knopf, 1985).

Sendak, Maurice. *Where The Wild Things Are.* (New York: Harper & Row, 1963).

Sendak, Maurice. *In The Night Kitchen.* (Weston, CT: Weston Woods).

Sendak, Maurice. *Outside Over There.* (New York: Harper & Row, 1981).

Spier, Peter. *Noah's Ark.* (Garden City, N.Y.: Doubleday, 1977).

Steig, William. *Doctor De Soto.* (Weston, CT.: Weston Woods Studios, 1983).

Steig, William. *Gorky Rises.* (New York: Farrar, Straus, Giroux, 1980).

Steig, William. *The Amazing Bone.* (New York: Farrar, Straus, Giroux, 1976).

Steig, William. *Brave Irene.* (New York: Farrar, Straus, Giroux, 1986).

Steig, William. *Amos & Boris.* (New York: Farrar, Straus, Giroux, 1971).

Steptoe, John. *The Story of Jumping Mouse.* (New York: Lothrop, Lee & Shepard Books,1984).

Steptoe, John. *Mufaro's Beautiful Daughters: An African Tale.* (New York: Lothrop, Lee & Shepard Books, 1987).

Thurber, James, illustrated by Louis Slobodkin. *Many Moons.* (New York: Harcourt, Brace & Company, 1943).

Turkle, Brinton. *Thy Friend Obadiah.* (New York: Viking Press, 1969).

Van Allsburg, Chris. *Jumanji.* (Boston: Houghton Mifflin Co., 1981).

Van Allsburg, Chris. *The Garden of Abdul Gasazi.* (Boston: Houghton Mifflin, 1979).

Van Allsburg, Chris. *The Polar Express.* (Boston: Houghton Mifflin, 1985).

Van Allsburg, Chris. *The Mysteries of Harris Burdick.* (Boston: Houghton Mifflin, 1984).

Stanley, Diane and Peter Vennema, illustrated by Diane Stanley. *Skaka King of The Zulus.* (New York: Morrow Junior Books, 1988).

Willard, Nancy, illustrated by Alice and Martin Provensen. *A Visit To William Blake's Inn: Poems For Innocent And Experienced Travellers.* (New York: Harcourt Brace Jovanovich, 1981).

Williams, Jay, illustrated by Mercer Mayer. *Everyone Knows What A Dragon Looks Like.* (New York: Four Winds Press, 1976).

Williams, Vera B. *A Chair For My Mother.* (New York: Greenwillow Books, 1982).

Williams, Vera B., illustrated by Vera B. and Jennifer Williams. *Stringbean's Trip To The Shining Sea.* (New York: Greenwillow Books, 1988).

Wood, Audrey, illustrated by Don Wood. *The Napping House.* (San Diego: Harcourt Brace Jovanovich, 1984).

Yagawa, Sumiko, illustrated by Suekichi Akaba. *The Crane Wife.* (New York: William Morrow, 1981).

Yolen, Jane. *Owl Moon.* (Weston, CT: Weston Woods, 1988).

Yorinks, Arthur, illustrated by Richard Egielski. *Hey, Al.* (New York: Farrar, Straus and Giroux, 1986).

Young, Ed. Lon Po Po: *A Red-Riding Hood Story From China.* (New York: Philomel Books, 1989).

Zelinsky, Paul. *Rumpelstiltskin.* (New York: E.P. Dutton, 1986).

Zemach, Margot. *It Could Always Be Worse.* (New York: Farrar, Straus & Giroux, 1976).

Zemach, Harve, illustrated by Margot Zemach. *Duffy and The Devil.* (New York: Farrar, Straus, Giroux, 1973).

# INDEX

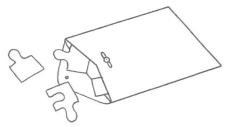